the
cleanse
companion
cookbook

the
cleanse
companion
cookbook

The Definitive Guide to the
Naturopathic Detoxification Diet
with 70 Hypoallergenic Recipes

Dr. Bonnie Nedrow, N.D.
Chef Jeff Hauptman

CONFLUENCE BOOKS
Ashland, Oregon

Confluence Books is an imprint of White Cloud Press

Confluence Books may be purchased for educational, business, or sales promotional use. For information, please write:

Special Market Department
Confluence Books
PO Box 3400, Ashland, OR 97520
Website: www.whitecloudpress.com

Cover and interior design by Confluence Book Services
Illustrations by Misty Stone
Author photo by Christy Collins

Printed in the United States of America

12 13 14 15 16   10 9 8 7 6 5 4 3 2 1

Library of Congress Cataloging–in–Publication Data

Nedrow, Bonnie, Dr.
The cleanse companion cookbook : the definitive guide to the naturopathic detoxification diet with 70 hypoallergenic recipes / written by Bonnie Nedrow and Jeff Hauptman.
    p. cm.
ISBN 978–1–935952–66–4 (pbk.)
1.   Detoxification (Health)––Recipes. 2.   Food allergy––Diet therapy––Recipes. 3. Nutrition. I. Hauptman, Jeff. II. Title.

RA784.5.N43 2012
641.5'63––dc23

2012014746

Acknowledgements

I want to thank all the staff at Hidden Springs for their enthusiasm and support during the creation of this book. I am especially appreciative of Brooks and Rod Newton for building this healing center, where over a dozen diverse practitioners collaborate to serve our community. I hope you will appreciate our book when cleansing and also anytime you want to enjoy abundantly healthy foods.

Special thanks to Kimberly Hall for attention to detail, Brooks Newton, Karen Caird and Chad Moyer for their literary feedback, to Beryl Jacobson for his artistic contribution, Rod Newton for seeing the potential and my husband Leo Balbuena for his constant support.

Dr. Bonnie Nedrow, ND

I would like to thank Dr. Bonnie Nedrow for the education and the opportunities that this book has brought me. Thank you Rod and Brooks Newton and the staff at Hidden Springs. Thank you Judy Blue and Steve Hauptman for your contribution in editing and assisting in the publication of this book. Also, a very special thank you to Dr. Bonnie Marsh, for our years of work together, and love and thanks to my son Tyler.

Chef Jeff Hauptman

Table of Contents

Introduction
Dr. Bonnie Nedrow, ND

I have been helping people optimize their health through metabolic cleansing for the past ten years. It is exciting to see the life changing effects of detoxification. I have seen many difficult cases become remarkably easier to treat or be resolved completely with cleansing alone.

The most challenging topic with the greatest number of questions and concerns for cleansers is, *'What do I eat'?* When I met Jeff, I was thrilled to find a chef who understands how to create wonderful tasting nutritious food within the context of detoxification.

I hope to demystify our recommended diet for cleansing while Chef Jeff provides scrumptiously satisfying food you will continue eating even when your cleanse is done.

Why would you love and cherish a cleanse cookbook? You may have participated in detoxification programs or fasting in the past and experienced or heard how restrictive and bland cleanse food is. In addition you are dreading starting your detox program because of all the yummy forbidden foods you will miss. While it is true you will be more limited in your food choices, we want you to experience cleansing foods that are delicious, flavorful, delightful to the eye, and satisfying on all levels.

Cleansing and detoxification programs have been part of nearly every culture and civilization since the dawn of humankind. All of these programs recommend the elimination or limitation of foods and food groups to decrease the burden on the body while our organs eliminate waste. We have two main ideas about cleansing diets which may diverge from what you have heard or tried in the past.

The first concept is to maintain a balance of macronutrients including fats, proteins, and complex carbohydrates in much the same ratios as those recommended in a healthy ongoing diet. We believe this is the key to keeping cleansing safe and to prevent re-toxifying our bodies as we detoxify. The second point we really want to drive home is that you should enjoy the flavorful diversity of the foods you eat.

So what is different about what you normally eat and what we recommend for cleansing? For some of you, not much will change in your food choices, while others will have major menu modifications. The basic foundation is an organic, whole foods, hypoallergenic, vegan diet. Whoa, that was a mouthful!

So what can you eat? We include an abundance of fresh raw or cooked vegetables, local fresh or frozen fruits, whole non-gluten grains, non-canned beans, lentils and peas (sprouted or cooked), whole raw or freshly roasted seeds, and herbal teas, spices, and natural flavors.

The substances we eliminate include caffeine, alcohol, sugar, animal products, and refined packaged foods. In addition, we recommend eliminating common inflammatory or allergenic foods such as wheat, corn, rye, spelt, barley, oats, potatoes, tomatoes, citrus, nuts, soy, eggplant, and peppers.

The recipes in this book are created to optimize the flavors and essence of cleansing foods. With the use of herbs, spices, and flavorings, as well as the variety of cooking methods described, simple vegetable, bean, and grain dishes become exotic tasting, satisfying, and nutritionally sound meals. By boldly experimenting with the wide selection of fresh, organic, whole, and healing foods, and seasonings suggested, you will develop a familiarity with the flavors and nutritional properties packed into nature's bounty. This will also help you in determining what tastes good to you. Even simple desserts and snacks will be satisfying and nutrient rich.

From raw to roasted, steamed to grilled, preparing these well-seasoned recipes will become a healthful adventure of limitless possibilities in *cleansing gastronomy*.

We are guessing that if you have found this book you understand the benefit of seasonal cleansing. We endorse periodic detoxification and want to assist you in safely removing toxins from your body with minimum risk. For a complete metabolic cleanse program, please visit the Hidden Springs website at www.hiddenspringswellness.com.

If you have not yet committed yourself to a detoxification program, you may be asking, *why would I want to submit myself to cleansing?* We live in a rapidly changing world where what we are exposed to in our food, our water, our air, and what touches our skin can bring about unpredictable effects to our health and vitality.

Ultimately, it is hoped that we can learn from past mistakes and find a feasible way to provide healthy non-toxic foods to people living in the modern world. However, clean energy, non-toxic packaging, and widespread use of non-polluting pesticides is a ways from reality.

In the meanwhile, we all need to find tools to protect our health, in spite of exposure to chemicals which can disrupt our endocrine systems and increase our risk of chronic illness. We hope this book helps you to eat good-tasting whole foods while you cleanse and that you learn new healthy ways to prepare the foods you eat all year.

This book is written to help you understand why some foods are eliminated while others are encouraged. While you may miss some of your comfort foods during your detoxification program, we hope you will enjoy the foods you do eat and find some new favorites to integrate into your yearlong nutritional habits.

Introduction
By Chef Jeff Hauptman

Since addressing my own health and weight issues several years ago, it has been my goal to educate and coach people in the importance of healthy cooking and eating.

In an effort to reduce my own risk of diabetes, I combined my culinary skills with a new understanding of food and health.

The Cleanse Companion Cookbook is a product of my experience as a professional chef along with an understanding of the importance of natural, whole, and healing foods required for optimum health. It is also an opportunity for me to showcase my simply prepared flavorful recipes that are also nutritionally sound. The collaboration of this book marks a very special time for me both personally and professionally.

The
Cleanse
Diet

What is Included

What is included in the cleanse diet? In short, it is a vegan whole food organic diet. It is well-balanced in protein, carbohydrates, and fats and packed full of phytonutrients and fiber. While there are some restrictions we encourage, there is a wealth of yummy healthy foods to choose from.

We realize that not all of you will have access to 100% organic foods, so we ask you to do your best. We also know that people are more willing to follow recommendations if they can really see the value, so this section is dedicated to helping you understand why the foods in this cookbook will assist your detox program.

Macronutrients

Macronutrients are carbohydrates, proteins, and fats. These three food groups are digested at different rates and provide different building blocks for the body's functions. They also provide fuel for energy.

We will start with carbohydrates as this group provides the greatest proportion: about 45% of the calories you need on a balanced diet. Carbohydrate-rich foods you can eat on a cleanse include vegetables, fruits, grains, and legumes. These foods provide fiber, vitamins, minerals, and phytonutrients. Carbohydrates are a great quick source of energy as they are digested rapidly.

Protein, comprising about 30% of our daily calories, is concentrated in legumes and seeds. Grains and vegetables also provide some of your needed proteins. Proteins have amino acids, which are the building blocks for muscles, immune cells, transport molecules, and enzymatic processes. In fact, the liver needs certain amino acids in order to rid the body of toxins. Proteins break down slower than carbohydrates helping to sustain energy for longer periods.

Fats are highly concentrated and only contribute about 25% of our daily calories. They get digested very slowly and help us feel satisfied when we eat a meal. Sources of fats include oils, olives, avocados, and seeds. Fats surround every cell in our body and are the building blocks for our hormones. They keep our skin soft and our joints mobile and are the main component of the brain. Our toxins are primarily stored in fats in the body, as well. During the cleansing process, fat is broken down and toxins are released, replacing the old unhealthy fats with fresh healthy ones.

Balance of Proteins, Fats, and Carbs

You may wonder why we are suggesting that you maintain a standard balance of macronutrients on a cleanse. You have probably read about or participated in detox programs, which involve fasting, juice–only, or vegetable–only diets. While these methods of detoxification have historically been a viable means of ridding the body of built–up waste, we believe that in the current environment of ever increasing toxins, a new model is called for.

A diet deficient in protein and fats has two potential risks. One is rapid weight loss with rapid loss of fat from storage. As fats are mobilized, toxins stored in those fats are released too quickly, overwhelming the body's ability to keep up with their elimination. The second concern is the loss of muscle mass in a low protein diet. If you are not eating protein daily, your body needs to borrow amino acids from somewhere. The richest storage of amino acids in the body is the muscles. Since most of us lose muscle mass as we age, we really can't afford to speed up that loss through detoxification.

Phytonutrients

Phytonutrients are not vitamins, minerals, or amino acids. They are substances produced by plants to protect themselves from the environment.

They repel pesky bugs, guard against cold and heat exposure, resist fungi, and help plants thrive against the odds. Organic foods are higher in phytonutrients because these plants live in a more stressful environment and have need for greater self–protection.

In humans, these less talked about nutrients are key in cell communication. They form complexes with proteins on the cell surface and send signals that impact cell function. In fact, they are critical to healthy gene expression.

Phytonutrients have been shown to decrease the risk of heart disease, cancer, arthritis, and diabetes. The take–home message is: when plants are forced to protect themselves, they produce nutrients which also help to protect humans.

Examples of phytonutrients include: **carotenoids** found in squash, yams, pumpkin, the cabbage family, spinach, apricots, peaches, cantaloupe, and watermelon; **flavonoids** found in blueberries, strawberries, raspberries, marionberries, onions and leafy greens; **phytates** found in whole grains and legumes; **indoles** found in broccoli, cabbage, Brussels sprouts, and cauliflower; **lignans** found in flaxseed, whole grains, seeds, apples, and cabbage; **phenols** found in green tea, coconut oil, olives, and berries; **saponins** found in alfalfa sprouts and ginseng; and **terpenes** found in thyme, rosemary, and peppermint.

As you can see, eating a good variety of organic fruits, veggies, grains, legumes, and herbs provides an abundance of health promoting phytonutrients. While most cleansing programs will recommend supplements to support the detox pathways, do not underestimate the power of whole organic foods to detox the body.

Fats

Fats are essential for lasting health. One of the most important functions of fat in a detoxification program is the building of cell membranes. The cell membrane is primarily made of fat. It is through this membrane that each cell is able to both bring in nutrients and remove waste. We want cell membranes to be flexible and permeable. This requires an influx of clean dietary fats to replace damaged old fats. A balance of healthy saturated fat, monounsaturated fat, and polyunsaturated fat will provide all the building blocks for a healthy membrane.

While many people believe that oils and fatty foods make you fat, this is not technically true. When including fat in your diet, be sure to remember that fat contains almost twice as much energy, or calories, per gram as do carbohydrates or proteins. In addition, oils do not have fiber or water in them, making them very compact. The take–home message is that a small amount of fat with each meal will enhance your health and increase your enjoyment without overburdening you with unneeded calories.

For cooking, we recommend virgin coconut oil. It has the advantage of remaining stable under relatively high heat. This means it will not become oxidized when cooked. Oxidization of oils can lead to damage to the fats in our cell membranes.

Coconut oil is rich in the medium chain triglyceride lauric acid, which is ready to be converted into energy by the liver rather than sent to fat storage. Lauric acid has also been shown to create an environment in the intestines in which good flora flourishes and bad flora is eradicated.

Adding flavor to food is one of the great properties of fats. Two healthy fats that taste fabulous are olive oil and toasted sesame oil. Sesame oil should be added at the end of the cooking process whereas extra virgin olive oil can be drizzled on after the meal is cooked or can be used for a low heat sauté. Flax and hemp oil also add flavor and should only be added after the cooking process is complete. Olives and avocados are another great source of healthy fat.

Some oils are labeled virgin or extra virgin. What does virgin and extra virgin really mean? Virgin refers to the way the oil is processed: it is a single cold pressing without the use of chemicals to extract the oil. Extra virgin refers to the quality of the olive oil including flavor, mouth feel, aroma, and acidity.

Fiber

Fiber prevents constipation, scrubs the surface of the bowel, and binds cholesterol and toxins, making it an invaluable aid to detoxification. It also slows down the absorption of glucose, helping to stabilize blood sugar. Our detox program includes a fiber supplement, but additional fiber in the diet is also important. Can you guess what food has the most fiber per gram? The most fiber is found in beans and other legumes, which contain over three times as much fiber as most fruits, vegetables, and grains.

Flavor and Fun

Flavor and fun are essential to eating. Just because you are cleansing, don't throw the baby out with the bath water!

Whole herbs and spices to be used freely are cumin, basil, bay leaf, tarragon, rosemary, oregano, thyme, fenugreek, fennel, cardamom, cinnamon, nutmeg, ginger, turmeric, black pepper, coriander, cilantro, clove, caraway, and mint. Flavorings include vanilla beans and vanilla and almond extract. Condiments include red or white wine vinegar, Umeboshi plum vinegar, apple cider vinegar, and balsamic vinegar.

Don't forget to enjoy your meals with family and friends. Even if your family chooses not to join you in your cleanse, they will be well-nurtured by the foods in this cookbook.

What Foods Should You Avoid?

What foods should you avoid during a detoxification program? It is essential that you eliminate anything which places an additional workload on the liver. These substances include sugar, caffeine, alcohol, recreational drugs, and over the counter medications. Any medications, herbs, or supplements you are on for the treatment of a medical condition should be continued.

People frequently ask if certain foods, which are not listed, are allowed. We have sorted and sifted through our combined knowledge of foods and have made an extensive list of foods we find to be nutritive and well tolerated by a majority of people.

We would encourage you to stick to our list and also to avoid any foods you know your body does not digest well. If you already have a very limited diet due to sensitivities and restrictions, you may benefit from working one-on-one with a nutritionist or naturopath.

If you have completed an in-depth elimination/challenge diet for food sensitivities in the past, some of the general restrictions can be lifted. We hope to give you a clear understanding of why we have chosen to include or disallow the foods on our diet so that you can consciously embrace these choices and intelligently modify them as desired.

Inflammatory Foods

Inflammatory foods are avoided in a cleansing program in order to optimize organ function. Toxins in our environment and the fats mobilized during a cleanse both contribute to inflammation. We want to keep the influx of dietary inflammatory foods at a minimum.

There are two basic sources of inflammation from our diet. The first is from arachidonic acid, the primary fat found in animal products. This fat feeds prostaglandin pathways causing inflammation in the body.

While an inflammatory response in the body is not always bad, during your detox it is important to down–regulate these pathways in order to rest the body. The second type of inflammatory food is food which we digest poorly. (See food intolerances below.)

Food Intolerances

Food intolerances or sensitivities can occur for three reasons. First, there may be a deficiency of an enzyme used to digest that food, as in lactose intolerance. Common foods with enzyme deficiencies are dairy and wheat.

The second type is a reaction to a toxin in or on the food from additives, contaminants, or natural chemicals in that food. Common toxic foods are non–organic foods, processed foods, and the nightshade family (see next page).

Finally there is an immune response, which may occur because we are over–exposed to a certain food. Note that an allergy to a food is also an immune response, but differs in that allergies have a rapid onset and are mediated by different immune cells. Common foods on the immune intolerance list are sugar, dairy, wheat, eggs, soy, nuts, citrus, fish, shellfish, chocolate, the nightshade family, and corn.

What does a food sensitivity reaction look like? The most common symptoms are fatigue, poor concentration, headache, rashes, diarrhea, constipation, irritable bowel, and an unproductive cough. Remember that these are delayed, not immediate reactions like allergies are. This means that a food eaten on Monday may not cause symptoms until Thursday.

As you can guess, it is nearly impossible to track reactions. For this reason, many people suffer from food intolerances but do not link their symptoms to their diet. On the cleanse, we take out the most common foods which cause reactions in the greatest number of people.

The Nightshade Family

The nightshade family is a common food group that causes immune reactions due to toxins produced by the plants. Joint pain is the most common symptom caused by this food family. The nightshades include potatoes, tomatoes, peppers, and eggplant. Yams and sweet potatoes are not nightshades.

Nuts

Nuts are a great source of healthy oils and easy protein. However, many people have a reaction to peanuts, which is really a legume, and to tree nuts including walnuts, almonds, cashews, pecans, hazelnuts, and Brazil nuts. Seeds are not a nut and can be eaten freely.

Citrus

Citrus is also not tolerated by many people, probably due to overexposure in our diet. Oranges are the most frequently intolerated in this family and should always be eliminated on a cleanse. Oranges also produce an excess of mucus, which can be congestive, especially for the nose.

Corn and Soy

Corn and soy are both foods that have been over–consumed, not only at the human table, but also in the grain troughs of the animals which provide food for humans including cows, pigs, chickens, turkeys, and farm–raised fish.

In addition, many sources of corn and soy are genetically modified. Over–consumption of one food stresses the body and, given time, a reaction occurs. Remember that variation and moderation bring health and happiness!

Gluten Grains

Gluten grains are particularly reactive and may trigger food sensitivity due to: a) an auto–immune reaction causing celiac disease, b) contamination of stored milled grains, and c) over–consumption with immune reactivity.

Grains in the gluten family are wheat, spelt, rye, and barley. Oats are not a gluten grain but are commonly packaged in the same facility as gluten grains leading to contamination. Buckwheat is not true wheat and is not in the gluten family.

The Other Top Allergens

The other top allergens are dairy, sugar, chocolate, eggs, fish, and shellfish. They are on the list because they commonly cause reactions in a large percentage of people. Dairy, sugar, and chocolate also lead to increased mucus and should be eliminated on a cleanse even if you tolerate them well otherwise.

Elimination/Challenge

Elimination/challenge refers to a process where you "eliminate" a food, or foods, completely from your diet for three weeks. At the end of that time you "challenge" a food by eating a good portion and waiting a few days to see if you have a reaction (see food sensitivity reaction above).

If you feel just as good after re–introducing an eliminated food, you tolerate that food and can include it on the list of healthy foods you eat regularly.

How to "Cheat" Intelligently

How to "cheat" intelligently is one of the most important concepts to grasp in order to be both successful and guilt-free on your detoxification program.

Do eat 7–9 half-cup servings of fruits and vegetables of a variety of colors every day. Do eliminate all white sugar, coffee, sodas, black tea, alcohol, and packaged foods with difficult to pronounce words on the label.

If you have done an elimination challenge in the past, and have found you do not react to nuts, nightshades, or citrus fruits, you could include these foods without fear of aggravation. Even if you haven't challenged them in the past, you may decide this is not the time to have such a restricted diet. You can always choose to challenge them in a future cleanse.

If giving up sugar completely seems too extreme, consider a small amount of honey or maple syrup.

If you must eat animal products, choose organic free-range meats, dairy and eggs, and make your portions small. Goat and sheep cheese, duck eggs, and lamb are all less allergenic choices.

If you have eliminated and challenged soy in the past and found no reaction, miso soup, wheat-free soy sauce, and tempeh could be included.

Corn meal, corn tortillas, breads, and flours tend to slow down digestion, so most people feel better without them even if they have challenged them successfully in the past.

Phase I and Phase II Detoxification

We won't go into great detail about the physiology of metabolic cleansing, but we would like to give you a basic understanding of the liver's role in detoxification.

It is the job of the liver to take fat-soluble toxins and convert them into water-soluble waste, which can exit the body in the form of bile or urine. This process is completed through enzyme pathways, which chemically change the molecule.

The two main enzyme pathways are called 'phase one' which occurs first, followed by 'phase two'. Both are important for successful cleansing.

However, phase two ends up being the most important because toxic molecules become free radicals after completing phase one. They then need to move to phase two in order to transform into benign waste.

Foods which support phase two are therefore emphasized on a cleansing diet and will be noted in the recipes that follow.

Happy Cooking and Cleansing!

Salads

Mixed Baby Green Salad
Tahini Vinaigrette

An abundance of leafy greens provides chlorophyll, an important detoxifier for the liver and a protective nutrient for all cells in the body.

- ☐ 6–8 cups seasonal mixed baby greens
- ☐ 1–2 cups of your favorite fresh sprouts
- ☐ 1 cup grated carrots
- ☐ 1 cup red cabbage, shredded
- ☐ 1 cup cucumber slices
- ☐ 1 Tbs raw sesame seeds

For the Dressing:

- ☐ 1/2 cup raw tahini
- ☐ 1/4 cup brown rice vinegar
- ☐ 2 Tbs green onion, finely chopped
- ☐ 1 Tbs fresh ginger, peeled and finely minced
- ☐ 1 clove garlic, finely minced
- ☐ 1/2 tsp ground cumin
- ☐ 1/2 tsp sea salt
- ☐ 1/4–1/2 cup water

1. Toss together all salad ingredients in a large bowl and set aside.

2. Place all of the dressing ingredients, except water, in a blender or mixing bowl. Blend or whisk adding only enough water to achieve desired consistency. Add more cumin or salt to taste.

3. Pour only enough dressing over salad to coat and toss. Top with more sesame seeds and serve.

Serves 4

Hearts of Romaine
with Avocado & Herb Dressing

Romaine lettuce is a great source of chromium, a nutrient essential for blood sugar stabilization. Erratic blood sugar is a stress on the body. During a cleanse it is optimal to protect yourself from unnecessary stressors.

- ☐ 2 heads Romaine lettuce, preferably hearts, washed and coarsely chopped
- ☐ 1 small head radicchio, torn into pieces, or 1 cup shredded red cabbage
- ☐ 1 cup fresh sunflower sprouts
- ☐ 2 Tbs raw sunflower seeds

For the Dressing:
- ☐ 2 medium size ripe avocados
- ☐ 2 cloves fresh garlic, finely minced
- ☐ 1/4 cup brown rice vinegar
- ☐ 2 Tbs Umeboshi plum vinegar
- ☐ 1/4 cup fresh herbs like basil, dill, parsley, cilantro or tarragon, coarsely chopped
- ☐ 1/4 – 1/2 cup water
- ☐ Sea salt and pepper to taste

1. Toss together all salad ingredients in a large bowl and set aside.

2. Place all of the dressing ingredients, except water, in a blender or mixing bowl. Blend or whisk adding only enough water to achieve desired consistency. Add more salt, vinegar, or herbs to taste.

3. Pour only enough dressing over salad to coat and toss. Top with more fresh herbs or sunflower seeds.

Serves 4

Cucumber & Wakame Salad

Seaweed is the single best source of iodine, a nutrient that is essential for thyroid health. Give your thyroid a boost by incorporating seaweed regularly in your diet.

- ☐ 2 medium to large cucumbers*, sliced lengthwise and then cut across into slices (about 4 cups)
- ☐ 1 small red onion, cut in half and then into thin slices (about 1 cup)
- ☐ 2–4 Tbs Wakame seaweed, soaked and drained according to package directions
- ☐ 1/4 cup flat leaf parsley, chopped
- ☐ 1/4 cup brown rice vinegar
- ☐ 2 Tbs Umeboshi plum vinegar
- ☐ 2–4 Tbs raw or toasted sesame oil
- ☐ 1/2 cup raw pumpkin seeds

1. In a large mixing bowl, toss together the cucumber, red onion, Wakame seaweed, and parsley. Add in the brown rice and Umeboshi vinegars and sesame oil.

2. Toss until vegetables are dressed. Add more of either vinegar or sesame oil to taste.

3. Turn salad into a serving dish and top with raw pumpkin seeds and more chopped parsley or Wakame seaweed.

* I prefer the Hothouse or English variety Cucumber.

Serves 4

Land & Sea
Grated Vegetable Salad

Daikon radish not only enhances flavor, it is also rich in digestive enzymes, helping us get the most nutritional value from our foods.

- ☐ 2 large carrots, peeled and grated (about 2 cups)
- ☐ 1 small celery root, peeled and grated (about 1 cup)
- ☐ 1 cup jicama, peeled and grated
- ☐ 1/2 cup Daikon radish, peeled and grated
- ☐ 2–4 Tbs Arame seaweed, soaked and drained according to package directions
- ☐ 1/2 cup chopped cilantro, dill, basil, chives, and/or flat leaf parsley
- ☐ 4 Tbs brown rice vinegar
- ☐ 2 Tbs Umeboshi plum vinegar
- ☐ 2–4 Tbs olive or sesame oil (optional)
- ☐ Scant tsp sea salt
- ☐ 2 Tbs black sesame seeds

1. In a large mixing bowl, mix all ingredients except sesame seeds. Toss to coat vegetables with vinegars, oil (if using) and herbs, adding more vinegar, herbs, or salt to taste.

2. Top with black sesame seeds and more fresh herbs and serve.

Colorful Vegetable Options *Include or substitute finely shredded green or red cabbage, or grated green or yellow zucchini.*

Serves 4

Sunflower Quinoa
& Vegetable Salad

Quinoa has more protein per ounce than any other grain. It tends to absorb the flavors of the foods you cook it with, making quinoa a great substitute for pasta. Try your favorite pasta dishes with quinoa instead.

- ☐ 2 cups cooked "Sunflower Quinoa" (see page 57)
- ☐ 1/4 cup olive oil
- ☐ 2–3 Tbs brown rice vinegar
- ☐ 1 medium cucumber*, diced (about 1 1/2 cups)
- ☐ 1 small red onion, diced (about 1/2 cup)
- ☐ 1 bunch fresh dill, chopped (about 1/4 cup)
- ☐ 1/2 tsp salt
- ☐ Black pepper to taste
- ☐ 1/4 cup sunflower seeds, raw or toasted

1. Place cooked quinoa in a large mixing bowl and gently turn in olive oil, vinegar, cucumber, onion, dill, salt, and pepper.

2. Add more vinegar, dill, or salt to taste.

3. Turn into serving dish and top with more fresh dill, and raw or toasted sunflower seeds.

* I prefer the Hothouse or English variety cucumber

Serves 4

Green Bean & Chickpea Salad

Chickpeas, also known as garbanzo beans, are a rich source of molybdenum, a nutrient essential for phase two liver function.

- ☐ 1 1/2 pounds fresh green beans, stem ends trimmed and cut in half (about 4 cups)
- ☐ 1 cup cooked chickpeas
- ☐ 1/4 cup olive oil
- ☐ 2 Tbs brown rice vinegar
- ☐ 1 Tbs fresh thyme leaves, chopped
- ☐ 1 Tbs whole toasted cumin seeds*
- ☐ 1/2 tsp salt and pepper to taste

1. Steam green beans for 3–4 minutes until crisp and tender and brightly colored.

2. Combine cooked green beans with the remaining ingredients and toss to combine and coat with dressing. Add a bit more oil or vinegar if desired and season to taste.

See Toasting Seeds, page 124

Asparagus also work well in this recipe.

Serves 4

Cannellini Bean Salad
with Mustard Seed Vinaigrette

> Mustard seeds are high in the phytonutrient glucosinolate which has been shown to have cancer protective benefits.

- [ ] 2 cups cooked Cannellini or other white beans, drained, reserving 1/4 cup cooking liquid for dressing
- [ ] 1 cup green and/or yellow zucchini, diced
- [ ] 1 cup fresh peas, or sugar snap peas, cut into small pieces
- [ ] 1 cup fresh fennel bulb, diced
- [ ] 1 cup grated carrot
- [ ] 1/2 cup green onions, coarsely chopped
- [ ] 1/4 cup flat leaf parsley, chopped

For the Dressing:
- [ ] 1/2 cup extra virgin olive oil
- [ ] 1/4 cup mustard seed vinegar*
- [ ] 1 Tbs vinegar soaked mustard seeds
- [ ] 1 small shallot, minced
- [ ] 1 clove garlic, minced
- [ ] 2 Tbs fresh basil, chopped
- [ ] Reserved bean cooking liquid or water
- [ ] 1/4 tsp sea salt and pepper to taste

1. Toss together all salad ingredients in a large bowl and set aside.

2. Place all of the dressing ingredients, except bean cooking liquid, in a blender or mixing bowl. Blend or whisk adding only enough liquid to achieve desired consistency. Add more vinegar, herbs, or salt to taste.

3. Pour only enough dressing over salad to coat and toss to combine. Add more salt and pepper to taste, if desired.

For the Mustard Seed Vinegar: Soak 1/4 cup yellow or brown mustard seeds in one cup white or red wine vinegar for at least 2 hours or overnight.

Serves 4

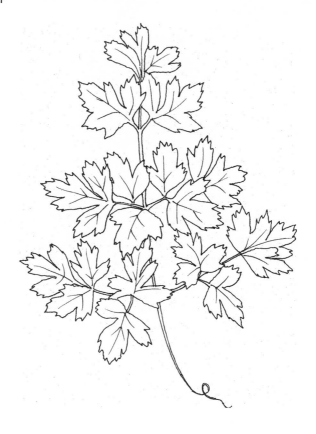

Cooked Vegetables

The Steamed Artichoke

The artichoke is a member of the thistle family, all of which protect and regenerate the liver. For folks with high cholesterol, this plant helps lower blood lipids.

Steaming the artichoke helps retain its nutrient content

☐ 1 medium to large globe artichoke per person
☐ 1 tsp brown rice vinegar per artichoke

Preparing the artichoke:

1. With a sharp knife, trim stem end and remove all the small bottom leaves. Do not cut stem completely off as it is an extension of the artichoke heart and is edible.

2. Cut about one inch from the top of the artichoke and discard pieces.

3. Using a scissor, trim the thorns off each artichoke petal.

4. Rub all cut surfaces with brown rice vinegar to prevent discoloration.

Cooking the artichoke:

1. Arrange artichoke(s), stem side up, in a steamer basket or insert placed in a heavy bottom stainless or enameled pot with tight fitting lid.

2. Add just enough water to come up to the level of the artichokes. Cover pot and gently steam until artichoke hearts are easily

pierced with a knife and the leaves pull off easily, about 35–45 minutes. Occasionally check the water level and add more if needed.

4. Allow artichoke(s) to cool slightly or chill before eating.

Eating the artichoke:

1. Pull off each leaf and, placing between your teeth, scrape the inner part of the leaf off. Discard the remainder of the leaf.

2. When the "heart" of the artichoke is left, scrape away and discard the fuzzy part, then cut the heart it into pieces.

Enjoy your artichoke with "Ginger and Kombu Hummus" (see page 101), "Savory Tahini Sauce" (see page 91), or your favorite vinaigrette.

Waterless* Cooked Vegetables

This is more of a cooking technique than a recipe. It is designed to preserve the natural flavors and the nutritional and therapeutic value of the vegetables. The beauty of this technique is that you can use any combination of colorful and seasonal vegetables. This recipe is derived from the book of Gerson Therapeutic Recipes.

Use 4–6 cups of any of the following vegetables:
- ☐ 1 large carrot
- ☐ 1 medium turnip
- ☐ 1 small celery root
- ☐ 1 medium parsnip
- ☐ 1 sweet potato
- ☐ 1 green and/or yellow zucchini
- ☐ 1–2 cups green beans, stem ends trimmed and cut in half
- ☐ 1–2 cups of cauliflower florets
- ☐ 1 red onion, peeled

1. Do not peel any of the vegetables (except the red onion), just wash and scrub them well and cut them into medium sized chunks.

2. Place cut vegetables in a large stainless pot with 1 inch of water and cover with a tight fitting lid.

3. Bring water to a simmer over medium heat. Turn heat down to low, cover pot, and slowly cook for 12–15 minutes or until vegetables are tender, occasionally checking on the water level and adding more if needed.

Serves 4

The term waterless refers to using only enough water to thoroughly cook the vegetables with little or no water remaining.

Tri-Colored Steamed Vegetable Medley

When the weather is cooler, raw foods can be a challenge to digest. Steaming vegetables supports digestion while preserving nutrients.

- ☐ 2 medium carrots, peeled and cut into 1 inch strips (about 2 cups)
- ☐ 2 medium parsnips, peeled and cut into 1 inch strips (about 2 cups)
- ☐ 1/2 pound green beans, stem ends trimmed and cut in half (about 2 cups)

1. Place the cut vegetables in a steamer basket or insert in heavy bottom stainless pot with a tight fitting lid. Add just enough water to come up to the level of the vegetables.

2. Cover pot and gently steam vegetables for about 5 to 7 minutes or until vegetables are crisp, tender, and brightly colored. Do not overcook.

As an alternative, you can cut the carrots into rounds and substitute broccoli and cauliflower florets for the parsnips and green beans.

Serves 4

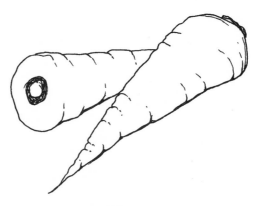

Balsamic Braised Leeks
& Napa Cabbage

Cabbage has long been used as a folk remedy for ulcers and other digestive complaints. It is healing and soothing for irritated and inflamed intestines and stomachs.

- ☐ 2–3 Tbs extra virgin olive oil
- ☐ 1 medium leek, washed thoroughly* and thinly sliced (about 2 cups)
- ☐ 2 cloves of garlic, minced
- ☐ 1 medium head of Napa cabbage, cut in half and thinly sliced (about 4 cups)
- ☐ 1/4 cup balsamic vinegar
- ☐ 1/2 tsp sea salt and pepper to taste
- ☐ 1/4 cup fresh basil leaves, cut into ribbons

1. Place a large stainless skillet, with a tight fitting lid, over medium–high heat.
2. Add the olive oil, the leeks, and salt. Sauté for 2–3 minutes until leeks are slightly wilted, but not browned.
3. Add the garlic and sauté 1–2 more minutes.
4. Add the cabbage, balsamic vinegar, salt, and pepper.
5. Reduce heat to low, cover skillet, and "braise" vegetables for 3–5 minutes or until the cabbage is wilted.
6. Toss in fresh basil and serve.

To clean leek: Cut off dark green portion and save for soup stock. Cut leek in half lengthwise and rinse under running water, making sure any sand or grit is removed. Pat dry and cut crosswise.

Serves 2–4

Seasonal Greens *with Fennel & Garlic*

Fennel not only adds great flavor, it also supports cleansing through regeneration of liver cells.

- ☐ 6–8 cups of loosely packed mixed "dark leafy" seasonal greens, such as spinach, Swiss chard, kale, mustard greens, or beet tops, washed and torn into pieces
- ☐ 2–3 Tbs olive oil
- ☐ 2 cups fennel bulb, thinly sliced
- ☐ 2–3 cloves garlic, minced
- ☐ 1 bunch green onions, trimmed and cut into 1–inch pieces
- ☐ 1/2 tsp salt
- ☐ 1 Tbs toasted fennel seeds*
- ☐ Pepper to taste

1. Place a large stainless skillet, with a tight fitting lid, over medium–high heat.

2. Add the olive oil, the fennel bulb, and salt. Sauté 2–3 minutes or until fennel is slightly wilted, but not browned.

3. Add garlic and green onions and sauté for 1–2 minutes more.

4. Stir in mixed greens, cover, reduce heat to low, and continue to cook for 2–3 minutes, until all greens are wilted, but remain bright green.

Top with toasted fennel seeds, a drizzle more olive oil, and salt and pepper to taste. For more tender greens, allow them to cook for 2–3 more minutes, being careful not to overcook them.

*See Toasting Seeds, page 124

Serves 4

Garlic Sautéed Broccoli Rabe

Garlic has retained a central role in 'kitchen medicine' as well as an indispensable herb for enhancing flavor in a wide array of recipes. It has been shown to reduce bad cholesterol, lower blood pressure, prevent infections, and protect against cancer.

- ☐ 2–3 Tbs olive oil
- ☐ 2–4 cloves garlic, thinly sliced
- ☐ 2 large shallots, or 1 small red onion, thinly sliced
- ☐ 2 pounds broccoli rabe*, stems trimmed and cut into 2–inch pieces (about 4 cups)
- ☐ 1/4 cup water
- ☐ 1/2 tsp sea salt
- ☐ pepper to taste

1. Place a large stainless skillet, with a tight fitting lid, over medium heat.

2. Add the olive oil, garlic, shallots, and salt and sauté for 1 minute, taking care not to burn.

3. Add the broccoli rabe and sauté for another 1–2 minutes.

4. Add the water, cover, reduce heat to low, and cook until broccoli rabe is wilted but remains bright green and crisp, about 2–4 minutes. Do not overcook.

5. Add more salt and pepper if desired.

If broccoli rabe is unavailable, substitute broccoli crowns cut into florets.

Serves 4

Zucchini Sauté *with Leeks & Basil*

Basil stimulates the gall bladder to increase the flow of bile. As bile is released, circulation to the liver is increased and detoxification pathways are supported.

- ☐ 2–3 Tbs extra virgin olive oil
- ☐ 1 medium leek*, cleaned and cut into 1/2 inch slices (about 2 cups)
- ☐ 4 medium green and/or yellow zucchini, cleaned and sliced into half moons (about 4 cups)
- ☐ 2–3 cloves of garlic, minced
- ☐ 1/4 cup fresh basil leaves, chopped
- ☐ 1 tsp yellow mustard seeds, lightly toasted (optional)
- ☐ 1/2 tsp sea salt
- ☐ Pepper to taste

1. Place a large heavy bottom skillet over medium–high heat.

2. Add the olive oil, leeks, garlic, and salt and sauté for 2–3 minutes or until leeks are slightly wilted but not browned.

3. Add the zucchini and sauté 2–3 more minutes or until zucchini is tender but still crisp.

4. Add the mustard seeds and basil and season with salt, pepper, and a drizzle of olive oil to taste.

Sliced red or white onion may be substituted for the leeks.

Serves 4

Steamed Sweet Potato Puree

> *Cumin is a fantastic digestive aid through stimulation of the pancreas. Cumin is also a powerful free-radical scavenger and enhances liver detoxification.*

- ☐ 2 medium–large sweet potatoes or yams, peeled and cubed (about 4 cups)
- ☐ 2 tsp ground cumin
- ☐ 1/2 tsp sea salt
- ☐ White pepper to taste

1. Place the cut sweet potatoes or yams in a steamer basket or insert in heavy bottom stainless pot with a tight fitting lid. Add just enough water to come up to the level of the vegetables.

2. Cover pot and gently steam vegetables for about 12 to 15 minutes or until vegetables are totally cooked through and soft.

3. Allow potatoes to cool slightly and transfer to a food processor. Add the cumin, salt, and pepper and process, in batches if necessary, until potatoes are pureed.

If a food processor is not available, potatoes can also be mashed in a bowl with a potato masher. Add more seasonings if desired.

Serves 4

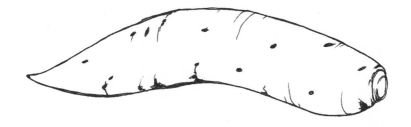

Shitake Mushroom & Sugar Snap Pea Stir–Fry

In Chinese medicine shitake mushrooms have traditionally been used to enhance kidney yang, which translates into increased vitality, longevity, and overall energy.

- ☐ 2–3 Tbs toasted sesame oil
- ☐ 1 small red onion, thinly sliced (about 1 cup)
- ☐ 1/2 tsp sea salt
- ☐ 1/2 pound fresh shitake mushrooms, stemmed and sliced (about 2 cups)
- ☐ 1 pound sugar snap peas, strings removed (about 2–3 cups)
- ☐ 1 Tbs fresh ginger, minced
- ☐ 1 Tbs toasted sesame seeds*

1. Place a large skillet or wok over medium–high heat.

2. Add the toasted sesame oil, the sliced onion, and salt. Stir–fry for 1–2 minutes until onions are slightly wilted but not browned.

3. Add the mushrooms and ginger and continue to stir–fry for 2–3 minutes more until mushrooms are cooked through and softened.

4. Add snap peas and stir–fry another minute or two until pea pods are tender, being sure to keep snap peas crisp and bright green.

5. Toss in toasted sesame seeds,* and, if desired, a drizzle more of the toasted sesame oil.

See Toasting Seeds, page 124

Serves 4

Provence Grilled Spring Vegetables

Asparagus has a high level of potassium, helping to eliminate toxins through the kidneys and bladder.

- ☐ 2 medium size leeks, trimmed, split lengthwise, and rinsed
- ☐ 4 medium size green and/or yellow zucchinis, cleaned and sliced in half lengthwise
- ☐ 1 pound asparagus, trimmed of fibrous ends
- ☐ 1 medium radicchio, cut into 4–6 wedges, with core intact
- ☐ 1/4 cup olive oil
- ☐ 2 Tbs Herbs de Provence (or a blend rosemary, marjoram, thyme, and lavender)
- ☐ 2–3 tsp sea salt
- ☐ Black pepper

1. Preheat grill to medium–high.

2. Toss vegetables with olive oil, Herbs de Provence, salt, and pepper.

3. Carefully grill each vegetable on all sides, turning frequently until slightly charred and tender, being careful not to burn.

4. Sprinkle with additional herbs, salt, pepper, and/or a drizzle of olive oil before serving.

Serves 4

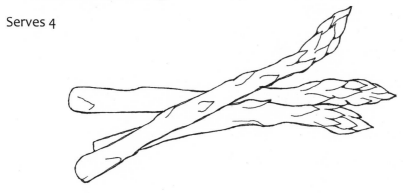

Coconut & Seed Roasted Vegetable Medley

Coconut oil is a rich source of medium chain fats, which are used primarily as an energy source and actually increase the body's metabolic rate, increasing energy and supporting weight loss.

- ☐ 3–4 Tbs coconut oil, melted
- ☐ 2 cups cauliflower florets
- ☐ 2 cups Brussels sprouts, trimmed and cut in half
- ☐ 2 cups butternut squash, peeled, seeded, and cut into cubes
- ☐ 1 medium red onion, large dice
- ☐ 2 Tbs raw "Seed Spice Blend" (see page 86)
- ☐ 1 tsp sea salt

1. Preheat oven to 375 degrees F.

2. Lightly oil baking sheet with 1 Tbs of the melted coconut oil.

3. In a large mixing bowl, toss the vegetables with the remaining coconut oil, seed blend, and salt.

4. Spread the vegetables in a single layer on the prepared baking sheet and bake for 25–35 minutes or until all the vegetables are cooked through, tender and golden. Carefully turn vegetables halfway through cooking.

Taste and add more salt and toasted ground seed blend, if desired.

Serves 4

Waterless Glazed Gingered Carrots

The detoxifying benefits of ginger include protection of the liver cells and antioxidant properties. Ginger also has the ability to increase circulation and move toxins out through the skin channel.

- ☐ 4 carrots, scrubbed and cut into 1/2 inch rounds (about 4 cups)
- ☐ 2 Tbs fresh ginger, finely minced
- ☐ 3–4 Tbs fresh dill, coarsely chopped
- ☐ 1 Tbs ground flax seeds
- ☐ 1/2 tsp sea salt (optional)

1. Place carrots, ginger, and flax seeds and about 1 inch of water in a medium size stainless sauce pot with a tight fitting lid.

2. Bring water to simmer over a medium heat. Turn heat down to low, cover pot, and slowly cook for 12–15 minutes or until carrots are tender but not overcooked.

3. Check the water level halfway through cooking, adding more if necessary.

4. Remove the lid and stir in dill, and salt if using.

5. Use the water and flax seeds at the bottom of the pot to "glaze" the carrots.

Beets and parsnips work well with or in place of the carrots.

Serves 4

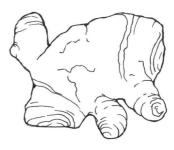

"Cured" Summer Squash
& Herb Fettuccini

Having a craving for pasta? Try this yummy vegetable substitute. You may not want to ever go back to wheat.

- ☐ 4–6 large green and/or yellow zucchinis, rinsed and ends trimmed
- ☐ 1 tsp ground coriander seeds
- ☐ 2–4 Tbs olive oil
- ☐ 1/2 cup chopped fresh summer herbs like parsley, basil, chives, cilantro, and/or tarragon
- ☐ Freshly ground black pepper
- ☐ Salt to taste

1. With a mandolin, box grater, or other slicing device, slice zucchini lengthwise into long narrow strips.

2. Toss the zucchini slices with salt and ground coriander seeds.

3. Place the mixture in a colander and allow zucchini to 'cure' for about 1 hour. The strips will exude water and become soft and pliable.

4. Squeeze excess water from the zucchini and toss "Zucchini Fettuccini" with enough olive oil to coat.

5. Add the fresh herbs and toss until combined. Add freshly ground black pepper and salt to taste, if desired.

6. Serve tossed with "Cilantro and Pumpkin Seed Pesto" (see page 90).

Serves 4

Balsamic Roasted Beets

Beets have a stimulating effect on the liver's detoxification process and additionally are a great remedy for constipation.

- ☐ 4 large beets, scrubbed and cubed (about 4 cups)
- ☐ 4 medium shallots, quartered
- ☐ 2–3 Tbs extra virgin olive oil
- ☐ 2–3 Tbs balsamic vinegar
- ☐ 1 Tbs Herbs de Provence
- ☐ 1/2 tsp granulated garlic
- ☐ 1/2 tsp sea salt
- ☐ 2 Tbs fresh mint, cut into ribbons

1. Preheat oven to 375 degrees F.

2. Lightly oil baking sheet with 1 Tbs olive oil.

3. In a mixing bowl, toss beets and shallots with remaining olive oil, vinegar, and seasonings except mint.

4. Place seasoned vegetables in a single layer on the prepared baking sheet and roast for 25–35 minutes or until beets are cooked through and tender. Carefully turn vegetables halfway through cooking.

5. Top roasted beets with fresh mint and a drizzle more balsamic vinegar and/or olive oil and serve.

Serves 4

Sesame Roasted Root Vegetables

> *While carrots have super antioxidant properties due to their high level of beta–carotenes, care must be taken to buy organically grown carrots as they easily absorb toxins from chemicals used in non–organic farming.*

6 cups of any of the following root vegetables, with peels on, scrubbed, and cut into even sized cubes:

- ☐ Turnips
- ☐ Parsnips
- ☐ Rutabaga
- ☐ Yam or sweet potato
- ☐ Carrot
- ☐ Red onion
- ☐ 3–4 Tbs toasted sesame oil
- ☐ 1–2 Tbs fresh ginger, finely minced or 1 tsp ground ginger
- ☐ 1/2 tsp black pepper
- ☐ 1/2 tsp sea salt
- ☐ 2 Tbs toasted sesame seeds

1. Preheat oven to 375 degrees F.

2. Lightly oil a baking sheet with 1 Tbs of toasted sesame oil.

3. In a large mixing bowl, toss cubed vegetables with seasonings and remaining oil.

4. Place the seasoned vegetables in a single layer on the prepared baking sheet and roast for 25–35 minutes, or until they are tender and a golden brown, turning halfway through the cooking.

5. Top with toasted sesame seeds.

Serves 4

Legumes

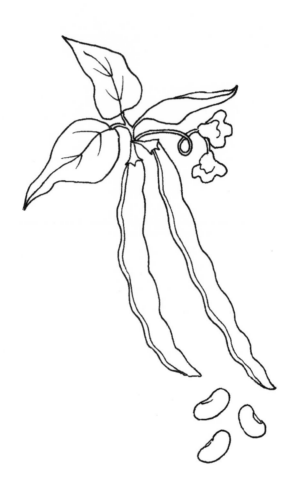

Basic Beans

Do you have challenges with erratic blood sugar? Try beans for breakfast to anchor your blood sugar early in the day. Experience less moodiness and less hunger all day long.

- ☐ 2 cups pinto, black, white, lima, navy, or other dried beans, soaked overnight and drained
- ☐ 2 generous slices of fresh ginger, unpeeled
- ☐ 2 large pieces Kombu seaweed
- ☐ 2 bay leaves
- ☐ 6 cups water
- ☐ 1 scant tsp salt

1. Place beans, ginger, Kombu seaweed, bay leaves, and water in a large stainless pot, with a tight fitting lid, and bring to a boil.

2. Reduce heat to low, cover pot and cook beans for 1 1/2 to 2 hours or until beans are tender and cooked through. Periodically check the water level adding more if needed.

3. Add the salt halfway through the cooking or only after beans have softened.

4. Allow mixture to cool, discarding only the bay leaves before using beans.

Use this method to cook any of the dried beans in recipes calling for "cooked beans."

Makes about 4 cups.

Re-fried Beans

Are beans hard for you to digest even after soaking and rinsing? Mashing beans breaks down their fibrous shell, reducing the gassy side effects of eating fiber rich legumes.

2 cups "cooked pinto beans" in their cooking liquid, including ginger and Kombu seaweed

- ☐ 1–2 Tbs olive oil
- ☐ 1/2 cup onion, minced
- ☐ 1 clove garlic, minced
- ☐ 1/2 tsp sea salt

1. Place a saucepan over medium heat, and add the olive oil, onions, and salt.

2. Sauté until onions are slightly wilted, but not browned and add the garlic. Sauté for 1–2 more minutes, and add the beans and a bit of the cooking liquid (include some ginger and Kombu seaweed) and mash until smooth with a potato masher.

3. Reduce heat to low and simmer, uncovered, for another 1–2 minutes or until desired consistency is reached.

4. The more liquid with the beans the longer it will take to cook down to a thicker consistency and the smoother the refried beans will be.

5. Leave the beans a bit on the runny side so you can dip your veggies in or cook them down as a yummy side dish with any root vegetable.

Serves 4

Lemongrass Lentils

Lemongrass has traditionally been used in Cuban folk medicine as an anti–inflammatory herb. During a cleanse, we encourage foods and spices which decrease inflammation and thereby support optimal organ function.

2 cups French lentils, picked–over, rinsed, and drained

- ☐ 2–3 Tbs coconut oil
- ☐ 1 medium onion, peeled and diced (about 1 cup)
- ☐ 1 medium carrot, peeled and diced (about 1 cup)
- ☐ 2 stalks celery, diced (about 1 cup)
- ☐ 2 cloves garlic, minced
- ☐ 1 Tbs fresh ginger, peeled and minced
- ☐ 1 large stalk lemongrass, use lower portion cut into 2 inch pieces and smashed flat to release flavor
- ☐ 1 scant tsp salt
- ☐ 5 cups water
- ☐ 1/2 cup chopped fresh herbs like parsley, basil, cilantro, or green onions for garnish and added flavor.

1. Place a soup pot, with a tight fitting lid, over medium–high heat.

2. Add coconut oil, onion, carrots, and celery and sauté for 2–3 minutes, stirring until vegetables are slightly wilted but not browned.

3. Add garlic, ginger, and lemongrass and sauté for 1–2 more minutes.

4. Add the lentils, salt, and water and bring to a boil. Turn heat to low, cover, and simmer lentils for 35–45 minutes or until lentils are cooked through and tender.

5. Before serving, remove large pieces of lemongrass and add fresh herbs and more salt, if desired.

Brown or green lentils may be substituted for the French lentils.

Spice Options: add mustard, cumin, fenugreek or fennel seeds to the pot along with the lemon grass.

Serves 4

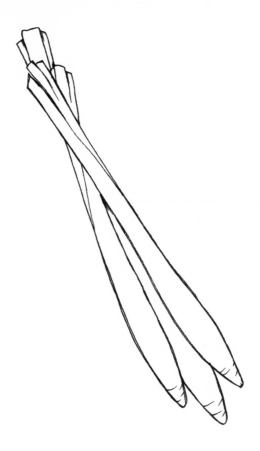

Baby Lima Beans *with Leeks & Spinach*

> *Do you want to receive the health benefits from garlic without eating garlic? Leeks have all the same healing properties as both garlic and onions with a sweeter, more subtle taste.*

2 cups "cooked baby Lima beans" with cooking liquid*

- ☐ 2 Tbs olive oil
- ☐ 1 large leek, split in half lengthwise, washed thoroughly and cut into 1/2 inch pieces
- ☐ 2 cups packed fresh spinach, washed thoroughly and coarsely chopped
- ☐ 1–2 cloves garlic, finely minced
- ☐ 1 Tbs fresh thyme leaves, chopped, or 1 tsp dried thyme
- ☐ 1/2 tsp ground turmeric
- ☐ 1/2 tsp salt
- ☐ 1/2 tsp white pepper
- ☐ 2 Tbs fresh chopped flat leaf parsley

1. Heat a large skillet over medium heat.

2. Add olive oil, leeks, and a pinch of salt and sauté for 2–3 minutes until leeks are wilted but not browned.

3. Add spinach, garlic, thyme, turmeric, and pepper and sauté 1–2 more minutes until spinach is wilted.

4. Stir in the cooked Lima beans along with some of the bean cooking liquid and bring the mixture to a simmer.

5. Stir in fresh parsley. Taste for seasoning and add a bit more salt, pepper and/or fresh herbs, if desired.

*See Cooking Beans, page 121

Serves 4

Black Beans with Burdock Root & Seed Spice Blend

> *Help the skin channel open and clear out toxins with burdock root. This tonifying food has been used historically for gentle liver and blood purification.*

- ☐ 2 cups dried black beans, rinsed, soaked overnight, and drained
- ☐ 2–3 Tbs coconut oil
- ☐ 1 small onion, diced (about 1 cup)
- ☐ 1 carrot, diced (about 1 cup)
- ☐ 2 stalks of celery, diced (about 1 cup)
- ☐ 1 large stalk burdock root, scrubbed and sliced
- ☐ 2 Tbs garlic, minced
- ☐ 2 Tbs ginger, minced
- ☐ 2 bay leaves
- ☐ 2 Tbs raw "Seed Spice Blend" (see page 86)
- ☐ 6 cups water
- ☐ 2 large pieces of Kombu seaweed
- ☐ 1 scant tsp sea salt
- ☐ Toasted & ground "Seed Spice Blend"
- ☐ Fresh chopped cilantro or flat leaf parsley
- ☐ Salt to taste

1. Place a large soup pot, with a tight fitting lid, over medium–high heat.

2. Add coconut oil, onion, carrot, celery, and burdock root and sauté for 2–3 minutes until vegetables are slightly wilted but not browned.

3. Add garlic, ginger, bay leaves, and raw "Seed Spice Blend" and sauté for 1–2 more minutes.

4. Add the soaked, drained beans, water, and Kombu seaweed and bring to a boil.

5. Reduce heat to low, cover, and simmer for 1 1/2 to 2 hours or until beans are cooked through and tender. Add salt halfway through cooking or only after beans have softened.

6. Before serving, season black beans with toasted and ground "Seed Spice Blend," fresh cilantro, or parsley and more salt if desired.

Serves 4

Basic Adzuki Beans *with Fennel*

> *Like chickpeas, adzuki beans are high in molybdenum,
> a nutrient essential to the sulfoxidation
> detoxification pathway in the liver.*

- ☐ 2 cup dried adzuki beans, rinsed and drained
- ☐ 1 small fennel bulb, thinly sliced (about 1 cup)
- ☐ 1 small yellow onion, thinly sliced (about 1 cup)
- ☐ 1 small carrot, thinly sliced (about 1 cup)
- ☐ 2 large pieces Kombu seaweed
- ☐ 2–3 slices fresh ginger
- ☐ 5 cups water
- ☐ 1 scant tsp salt
- ☐ 1 Tbs toasted and ground fennel seeds
- ☐ 1 Tbs green onion, chopped

1. Place the adzuki beans, fennel, onion, carrot, Kombu, ginger, and water in a large soup pot, with a tight fitting lid, and bring to a boil.

2. Cover, turn heat to low, and simmer for about 1–1 1/2 hours, or until beans are cooked through and tender. Add salt halfway through cooking or only after beans have softened.

3. Sprinkle toasted ground fennel seeds and green onions on top of cooked beans for added flavor.

Serves 4

Black–Eyes Peas *with Mirepoix*

Black–eyed peas are the highest vegetarian source of folate. Folate is one of the essential nutrients needed to complete methylation, a detox pathway which removes heavy metals.

- ☐ 2 cups dried black–eyed peas, rinsed and drained
- ☐ 2–3 Tbs olive oil
- ☐ 2 cups diced onion
- ☐ 1 cup diced carrot
- ☐ 1 cup diced celery
- ☐ 1 Tbs minced garlic
- ☐ 2 bay leaves
- ☐ 2–3 1 inch pieces of Kombu seaweed
- ☐ 2–3 slices fresh ginger
- ☐ 1 Tbs dried Herbs de Provence
- ☐ 6 cups water
- ☐ 1 scant tsp sea salt

1. Place a large stainless soup pot, with a tight fitting lid, over medium–high heat.

2. Add the olive oil and the Mirepoix mix of onions, carrot, and celery and sauté for 2–3 minutes until vegetables are slightly wilted but not browned.

3. Add garlic and sauté for another minute.

4. Add drained black–eyed peas, bay leaves, Kombu seaweed, ginger, Herbs de Provence, and water and bring to a boil.

5. Reduce heat to low, cover and simmer for about 1 to 1 1/2 hours or until peas are tender and cooked through. Add salt halfway through cooking or only after beans have softened.

6. Taste for seasoning and add a bit more salt, pepper, and/or herbs, if desired. Remove bay leaves before serving.

Serves 4

Grains

Basic Millet

Although cooked and eaten like a grain, millet is actually a seed, packed with vitamins and minerals. It is particularly high in magnesium, a mineral essential to most detoxification pathways.

☐ 1 cup millet
☐ 2 cups water
☐ 1/2 tsp sea salt

Wash millet and drain through fine mesh strainer.

1. In a medium sized pot with a tight fitting lid, bring water and salt to a boil.

2. Add rinsed millet and return to a boil.

3. Turn heat to low and cover and cook at a simmer for 30–35 minutes or until all the water is absorbed.

4. Allow cooked millet to rest 5 more minutes before removing lid.

5. Fluff with a fork before using.

Makes about 3 cups.

Cooked millet can be served with "Savory Tahini Sauce" (see page 90) or in "'Millet'strone Soup" (see page 72).

Brown Rice *with Amaranth*

> *Amaranth is particularly high in methionine, an amino acid, which is a precursor for glutathione. Glutathione is an important nutrient required for phase one liver detoxification.*

- ☐ 1 cup short grain brown rice
- ☐ 1/4 cup Amaranth
- ☐ 2 1/2 cups water
- ☐ 1/2 tsp sea salt

1. Place the rice, Amaranth, water, and salt in a medium pot with a tight fitting lid.

2. Bring to a boil, cover and reduce heat to low. Simmer for 45–55 minutes or until all the water has been absorbed and rice is cooked through. Do not stir during cooking.

3. Turn off heat and leave covered for 10 more minutes before serving.

4. For added flavor and nutrition add 1 tsp fenugreek, cumin, mustard, and/or fennel seeds to rice before cooking.

Makes about 3 cups

Sunflower Quinoa

Turmeric is a fantastic detox herb in that it slows phase one detox pathways while stimulating phase two pathways. This feature is important when there is a need to remove cancer–causing compounds in the liver.

- ☐ 1 cup quinoa
- ☐ 1/4 cup sunflower seeds
- ☐ 1 tsp fenugreek seeds (optional)
- ☐ 2 1/4 cups boiling water
- ☐ 1/2 tsp salt
- ☐ 2 tsp minced fresh turmeric or 1/2 tsp ground turmeric

1. Place quinoa and sunflower seeds and fenugreek seeds in a stainless pot over medium heat and dry toast for 2 to 3 minutes, until seeds begin to pop and quinoa is lightly browned, stirring frequently so as not to burn the seeds.

2. Remove pot from heat and very carefully* add the boiling water and then the salt and turmeric.

3. Place pot back over heat, return to a simmer, cover and cook over low heat for 20 minutes.

4. Turn off heat and leave pot covered for 10 more minutes before removing the lid.

5. Fluff with fork and serve.

Exercise extreme caution when adding the boiling water to the hot pot. Remove the pot from the heat, and add the water quite slowly until all sputtering has stopped.

Spice options: *A small pinch of saffron can be added in place of the turmeric, or substitute cumin, fennel, or mustard seeds in place of the fenugreek seeds.*

Serves 4

Sesame & Shitake Buckwheat

While it sounds like a type of wheat, buckwheat is actually a hypoallergenic seed. It cooks much like a grain and as such is enjoyed as a side dish served with vegetables and legumes.

- ☐ 1 cup toasted buckwheat groats
- ☐ 2 Tbs white or hulled sesame seeds
- ☐ 2 1/2 cups boiling water
- ☐ 1/2 tsp sea salt
- ☐ 1/2 cup dried shitake or other dried mushrooms
- ☐ 2 Tbs toasted sesame oil

1. Place buckwheat groats and sesame seeds in a stainless pot over medium heat and dry toast for 2 to 3 minutes or until seeds begin to pop and buckwheat becomes aromatic, stirring frequently so as not to burn the seeds.

2. Remove pot from heat and very carefully* add boiling water and the salt.

3. Place pot back over low heat and add dried shitake mushrooms, cover and cook for 20 minutes.

4. Turn off heat and leave covered for 10 more minutes.

5. Fluff with fork and drizzle with toasted sesame oil and serve.

Exercise extreme caution when adding the boiling water to the hot pot. Remove the pot from the heat, and add the water quite slowly until all sputtering has stopped.

Serves 4

Seeded Teff Polenta

Teff is a highly nutritious grain composed primarily of bran and germ. The bran in grains provides their fiber content while the germ in grains is where Vitamin E and the B Vitamins are found. B Vitamins are essential to phase one detoxification in the liver.

- ☐ 1 cup Teff
- ☐ 2 1/2 cups boiling water
- ☐ 1/2 tsp sea salt
- ☐ 1/4 cup of any of the following seeds: pumpkin, sunflower, sesame, and/or flax

1. In a medium pot, bring water and salt to a boil. Add Teff and stir.

2. Return to a boil, reduce heat to low, cover, and simmer for 20–30 minutes.

3. Stir pot occasionally throughout cooking and cook until all the water is absorbed and Teff is creamy.

4. Stir in the seeds.

Teff "Polenta" can be enjoyed at this point or poured into a heat-proof dish and cut into slices when cooled. Teff is also nice as breakfast porridge topped with fresh berries.

Serves 4

Lovely Lynna's Rice and Lentils

Lentils as a member of the legume family have been shown to not only lower cholesterol but also improve the ratio of good to bad cholesterol.

- ☐ 1 cup short grain brown rice
- ☐ 1/2 cup brown lentils, soaked for 2–4 hours, and drained
- ☐ 3 ¾ cups water
- ☐ 1 tsp salt

1. Place all the ingredients in a stainless pot with a tight fitting lid.

2. Bring to a boil, cover, and reduce heat to low.

3. Cook rice and lentils for about 1 hour or until all the water is absorbed and lentils are cooked through and tender.

For added flavor and nutrition, add 1 Tbs mustard, cumin, and/or fenugreek seeds to the pot while cooking.

Serves 4

Soups

Potassium Broth

This is a great recipe to make during the deeper phase of your cleanse program. It can be sipped on throughout the day to increase energy when your diet is a bit light.

- ☐ 2 large carrots, unpeeled, scrubbed, and roughly chopped
- ☐ 1 large onion, roughly chopped, include peel
- ☐ 2–4 celery ribs, tops and all, washed and roughly chopped
- ☐ 1 medium celery root, unpeeled, scrubbed, and roughly chopped
- ☐ 1 medium turnip, unpeeled, scrubbed, and roughly chopped
- ☐ For additional flavor and nutrition also recommended are: kale or parsley leaves and stems, fresh garlic (include peel), ginger, thyme, and/or Kombu seaweed.

1. Place all or any of the above vegetables and flavorings in a large stainless steel soup pot and add cold filtered water to cover vegetables.

2. Bring the mixture to a boil and cover.

3. Reduce heat to low and simmer for 30–40 minutes, or until all the vegetables are tender and cooked through and the broth is flavorful.

Allow to cool and strain.

Makes about 6 cups

Chilled Cucumber
& Avocado Soup

Avocados are very rich in potassium which alkalizes the urine, assisting the kidneys in pulling out toxins. They also contain the phytonutrient beta–sisterol which has cholesterol–lowering and anti–cancer effects.

- ☐ 4 large cucumbers, peeled or not, and cubed
- ☐ 2 avocados, peeled and pit removed
- ☐ 2 Tbs fresh ginger, peeled and minced
- ☐ 1/2 cup fresh basil, parsley, chives, and/or other fresh leafy herbs, chopped
- ☐ 2–4 Tbs brown rice vinegar
- ☐ 1 Tbs ground cumin
- ☐ 1 tsp sea salt
- ☐ White pepper to taste
- ☐ 1 Tbs raw or toasted cumin seeds* for garnish

1. In a blender or food processor, puree all ingredients (in batches if necessary) until smooth and creamy. Process less for a chunkier soup.

2. Taste and add more vinegar, salt, or pepper if desired.

3. Chill and serve topped with cumin seeds and/or more fresh herbs.

*See Toasting Seeds, page 124

Serves 4–6

Creamy Cauliflower
& Celery Root Soup

Cauliflower is in the cruciferous vegetable family which activates phase two liver detox pathways and so speeds up detoxification and reduces the risk of a build up of toxic intermediates.

- ☐ 2 Tbs olive oil
- ☐ 1 small leek, washed thoroughly and coarsely chopped
- ☐ 1 small onion, diced (about 1 cup)
- ☐ 1 small head of cauliflower, cut into chunks (about 2–3 cups)
- ☐ 2 cups celery root, peeled and cubed (or 2 cups celery, diced)
- ☐ 1 Tbs fresh thyme leaves or 2 tsp dried
- ☐ About 6 cups of "Potassium Broth" (see page 63) or water
- ☐ 1 tsp sea salt
- ☐ 1/2 tsp white pepper
- ☐ 2 Tbs snipped chives for garnish

1. Heat olive oil in large soup pot over medium heat.

2. Add leek and onion and sauté for 2–3 minutes until vegetables are coated with oil and slightly softened, but not browned.

3. Add the celery root (or the celery) the cauliflower and the thyme and stir to combine vegetables.

4. Add enough broth or water to cover vegetables by about an inch. Add sea salt and pepper.

5. Bring to a boil, cover pot, and lower heat to simmer.

6. Cook for about 20–35 minutes, or until vegetables are cooked through and tender.

7. Allow mixture to cool slightly and transfer to a blender. Puree in batches until all is blended.

8. Return puree to the soup pot and gently reheat over low heat. Taste for seasoning and add more herbs, salt, or pepper if desired. Serve topped with snipped chives.

Serves 4

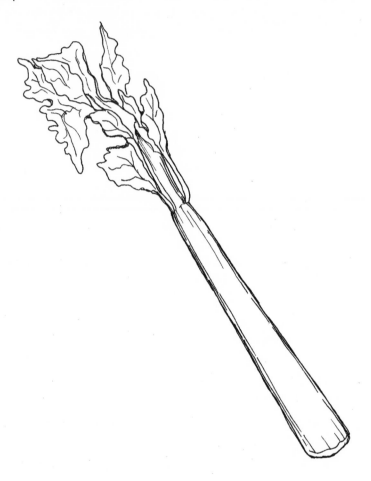

Winter Squash & Jerusalem Artichoke Soup

Jerusalem artichokes are one of the richest sources of inulin, a starch that provides a favorable environment in the intestines for good bacteria to thrive.

- ☐ 2–3 Tbs olive oil
- ☐ 1 onion, diced (about 2 cups)
- ☐ 1 carrot, diced (about 2 cups)
- ☐ 1 medium butternut or other winter squash, peeled, seeded, and cubed (about 4 cups)
- ☐ 2 cups Jerusalem artichokes, scrubbed and chopped
- ☐ 2 Tbs fresh ginger, minced
- ☐ 1 Tbs fresh turmeric, minced, or 1 tsp ground
- ☐ 1 Tbs fresh garlic, minced
- ☐ 1 tsp fenugreek seeds
- ☐ 6–8 cups "Potassium Broth" (see page 63) or water
- ☐ 1 tsp sea salt
- ☐ Pepper to taste

1. Heat olive oil in a large soup pot over medium–high heat.

2. Add the onion, carrot, cubed squash, Jerusalem artichokes, and salt. Sauté for 2–3 minutes until vegetables are slightly wilted but not browned.

3. Add the ginger, turmeric, garlic, and fenugreek seeds and stir to coat vegetables with the spices.

4. Add the "Potassium Broth" (or water) and bring to a boil. Reduce heat to a simmer and cook until the vegetables are cooked through and tender.

5. Taste and add more salt or pepper if desired.

6. If a creamy soup is desired, puree in a blender until smooth.

Serves 6

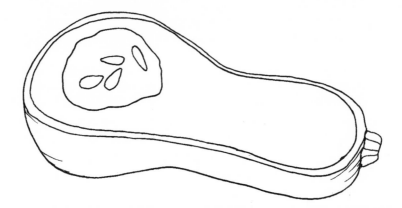

Golden Vegetable & Seed Milk Soup

> *Spinach is high in a broad array of phytonutrients and has been shown to be particularly protective against all types of cancer.*

- ☐ 3–4 Tbs coconut oil
- ☐ 1 Tbs fresh ginger, peeled and minced
- ☐ 1 Tbs fresh garlic, minced
- ☐ 1 Tbs curry powder
- ☐ 1 Tbs "Seed Spice Blend" (see page 86)
- ☐ 1 small onion, sliced thinly (about 1 cup)
- ☐ 1 carrot, sliced on diagonal (about 1 cup)
- ☐ 1 parsnip, sliced on diagonal (about 1 cup)
- ☐ 1 small fennel bulb, sliced thinly (about 1 cup)
- ☐ 2 cups butternut or other hard–shelled squash, peeled, seeded, and cubed
- ☐ 6 cups "Pumpkin and Sunflower Seed Milk" (see page 92) or water
- ☐ 2 cups loosely packed fresh spinach
- ☐ Salt and pepper to taste.

1. Heat coconut oil in a large soup pot over medium heat.

2. Add the ginger and garlic and sauté for 1–2 minutes.

3. Add curry powder, "Seed Spice Blend," and all the vegetables, except spinach. Stir until the vegetable mixture is coated with the oil and spices and cook for another 3–4 more minutes.

4. Add the "Pumpkin and Sunflower Seed Milk" or water and bring to a boil. Cover pot, reduce heat to a simmer and cook for 20–25 minutes or until vegetables are tender and cooked through. Toss in the spinach and cook until wilted.

5. Season with more curry powder and/or salt and pepper to taste.

Serves 6

Brown Rice &
Toasted Sesame Soup

Short grain brown rice has superior nutrition to other varieties of rice due to its high bran content.

For the Sesame Rice:
- ☐ 1 cup short grain brown rice
- ☐ 1/4 cup hulled or white sesame seeds
- ☐ 1/2 tsp sea salt
- ☐ 2 1/2 cups water

1. Place the rice, sesame seeds, salt, and water in saucepan.

2. Bring to a boil, reduce heat to a simmer, and cover with a tight fitting lid.

3. Cook rice for 45–55 minutes or until water is absorbed and rice is done. Allow rice to rest 10 minutes before lifting the lid. Set aside for soup.

For the soup:
- ☐ 3–4 Tbs toasted sesame oil
- ☐ 1 small onion, diced (about 1 cup)
- ☐ 2 celery stalks, diced (about 1 cup)
- ☐ 1 carrot, diced (about 1 cup)
- ☐ 1/2 tsp sea salt
- ☐ 2 cups cooked Sesame Rice
- ☐ 4–6 cup "Potassium Broth" (see page 63) or water
- ☐ 1 Tbs fresh or 1 tsp dried thyme leaves
- ☐ 2 Tbs green onions, chopped
- ☐ 1 Tbs fresh parsley, chopped
- ☐ 2 Tbs toasted sesame seeds for garnish

1. Heat the sesame oil in a large soup pot, over medium heat.

2. Add the onion, celery, carrot, and salt, and sauté vegetables for 2–3 minutes until slightly wilted, but not browned.

3. Add cooked Sesame Rice, "Potassium Broth" or water, and thyme.

4. Bring mixture to a boil, reduce heat, and simmer for 10–12 minutes more or until vegetables are soft and cooked through.

5. Taste and add more thyme, salt, and/or pepper if desired.

Soup is ready at this point or can be pureed by carefully transferring cooled soup in small batches to blender and blending until smooth. Return blended soup to pot and gently return to a simmer, stirring occasionally.

Garnish with green onion, parsley, and toasted sesame seeds.

Serves 6

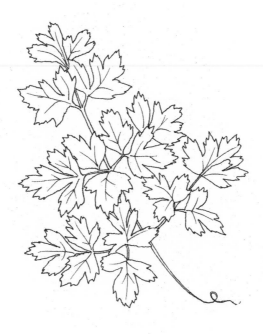

'Millet'strone Soup

- ☐ 2–3 Tbs olive oil
- ☐ 1 small onion, diced (about 1 cup)
- ☐ 1 carrot, diced (about 1 cup)
- ☐ 2 stalks of celery, diced (about 1 cup)
- ☐ 1/2 tsp sea salt
- ☐ 2 Tbs minced garlic
- ☐ 2 Tbs minced ginger
- ☐ 2 Tbs fresh oregano or 2 tsp dried
- ☐ 2 bay leaves
- ☐ 1 medium zucchini, diced (about 2 cups)
- ☐ 2 cups green beans, stem ends trimmed and beans cut into 1 inch pieces
- ☐ 2 cups cooked kidney beans, drained (see basic bean cooking)
- ☐ 6 cups "Potassium Broth" (see page 63) or water
- ☐ 1–2 cups "Basic Millet" (see page 55)
- ☐ 1 bunch flat leaf parsley, washed and chopped
- ☐ Salt, pepper, and dried herbs for seasoning

1. Heat olive oil in large soup pot over medium heat.

2. Add onion, carrot, celery, and salt and sauté for 2 to 3 minutes, until the vegetables are slightly wilted but not browned.

3. Add the garlic, ginger, oregano, and bay leaves and sauté for 1–2 minutes more.

4. Add zucchini, green beans, kidney beans, and the broth or water. Bring mixture to a boil, reduce heat, and cook for 15–20 minutes or until all the vegetables are tender and cooked through.

5. Stir in the millet and parsley and bring soup back to a boil.

6. Remove bay leaves before serving.

Taste and season soup with more herbs, salt, and/or pepper if desired.

Serves 6

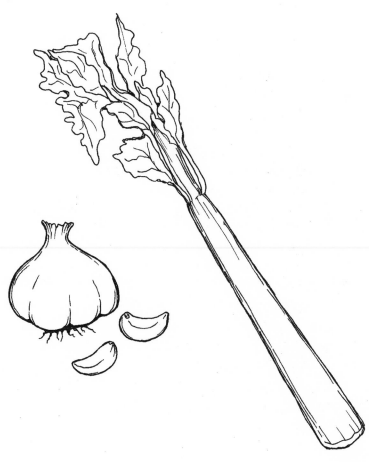

Land & Sea White Bean Puree

> *Want to eat your way to a healthier immune system?*
> *Include plenty of oregano and thyme in your diet,*
> *both of which provide good protection*
> *from viruses, yeast, and parasites.*

- ☐ 2 cups dried Great Northern or any other white bean, rinsed and soaked overnight and drained
- ☐ 2–3 Tbs olive oil
- ☐ 1 large onion, rough chopped
- ☐ 1 large carrot, rough chopped
- ☐ 2 stalks of celery, rough chopped
- ☐ 2 Tbs minced garlic
- ☐ 2 Tbs minced ginger
- ☐ 2–3 Tbs dried Italian Herb Blend or Herbs de Provence
- ☐ 2–3 1 inch pieces of Kombu seaweed
- ☐ 6–8 cups "Potassium Broth" (see page 63) or water
- ☐ 2 tsp sea salt
- ☐ 1 bunch flat leaf parsley, washed and chopped
- ☐ Salt, pepper, and more dried herbs for seasoning

1. Heat olive oil in large soup pot over medium heat.

2. Add onion, carrot, and celery. Sauté for 2–3 minutes until vegetables are slightly softened, but not browned.

3. Add garlic and ginger and sauté for 1–2 more minutes.

4. Add the white beans, dried herbs, Kombu seaweed, and the broth or water. Stir well and bring mixture to a boil. Cover and reduce heat.

5. Cook for 1 1/2 – 2 hours, or until the beans are cooked through and tender. Allow beans to cool. Add salt halfway through cooking or only after beans have softened.

6. Working in batches, carefully puree soup in a blender until smooth and return to pot.

7. Gently bring puree to boil, adding more broth to thin if necessary. Season with salt, pepper, chopped parsley and more dried herbs to taste.

Serves 6

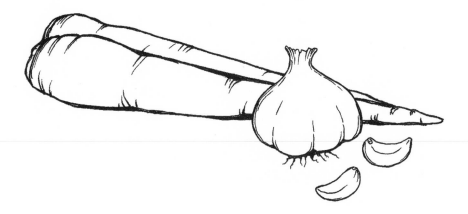

Red Lentil & Rosemary Soup

- ☐ 2–3 Tbs olive oil
- ☐ 1 medium onion, peeled and diced (about 1 cup)
- ☐ 1 large carrot, peeled and diced (about 1 cup)
- ☐ 2 cloves garlic, minced
- ☐ 2 Tbs fresh ginger, peeled and minced
- ☐ 1–2 Tbs fresh or 2 tsp dried, rosemary leaves, chopped
- ☐ 2 cups red lentils, rinsed and drained
- ☐ 6–8 cups "Potassium Broth" (see page 63) or water
- ☐ 1–2 tsp sea salt
- ☐ Pepper to taste
- ☐ 1 Tbs minced fresh chives (optional)

1. Heat olive oil in a soup pot over medium–high heat.

2. Add onion and carrot and sauté for 2–3 minutes until vegetables are slightly wilted, but not browned.

3. Add garlic, ginger, and rosemary and continue to sauté for 1–2 more minutes.

4. Add rinsed lentils and broth or water to the vegetables and bring to a boil.

5. Reduce heat to low, cover, and simmer for about 40–50 minutes or until the lentils and vegetables are cooked through and tender.

6. Add salt, pepper, and/or more rosemary to taste.

For a creamy soup, allow mixture to cool slightly and transfer to a blender. Blend in small batches, if necessary, until mixture is pureed.

Gently reheat before serving and garnish with chives.

Serves 6

Split Pea Fennel & Herb Soup

Have you always seen celery as simply a crunchy food low in calories? Celery is a great cleanse food as it supplies an abundance of potassium, a nutrient which alkalizes the urine, helping the kidneys filter out waste.

- ☐ 2–3 Tbs olive oil
- ☐ 1 medium fennel bulb, trimmed, diced (about 2 cups)
- ☐ 1 small onion, diced (about 1 cup)
- ☐ 2 stalks celery, diced (about 1 cup)
- ☐ 2 cloves of garlic, minced
- ☐ 2 Tbs fresh ginger, minced
- ☐ 1 Tbs fresh turmeric, minced or 1 tsp dried
- ☐ 2 cups green split peas, rinsed and drained
- ☐ 6–8 cups "Potassium Broth" (see page 63) or water
- ☐ 2 tsp fresh thyme leaves
- ☐ 2 bay leaves
- ☐ 1–2 tsp sea salt
- ☐ Pepper to taste
- ☐ 1 Tbs toasted fennel seeds (optional)

1. Heat olive oil in soup pot over medium–high heat.

2. Add the fennel, onion, and celery. Sauté for 2–3 minutes until vegetables are slightly wilted, but not browned.

3. Add garlic, ginger, and turmeric and continue to sauté for 1–2 more minutes.

4. Add rinsed split peas, , or water, thyme, and bay leaves and bring the mixture to a boil.

5. Reduce heat to low, cover, and simmer for about 40–50 minutes or until split peas and vegetables are cooked through and tender, stirring occasionally.

6. Add the salt and pepper to taste.

7. Before serving, remove the bay leaves and top with toasted fennel seeds.

8. For a creamy soup, allow mixture to cool slightly and transfer to a blender. Blend in small batches, if necessary, until mixture is pureed.

Serves 6

Curried Winter Squash Stew
with Chickpeas

> *Do you suffer from food sensitivities and/or environmental allergies? Eat plenty of quercetin rich onions to help heal your gut and decrease the histamine response.*

- ☐ 2–3 Tbs coconut oil
- ☐ 1 medium onion, coarsely chopped (about 1 cup)
- ☐ 1 carrot, coarsely chopped (about 1 cup)
- ☐ 2 stalks of celery, coarsely chopped (about 1 cup)
- ☐ 1 medium butternut or other winter squash, peeled, seeded and cubed (about 3–4 cups)
- ☐ 1–2 Tbs fresh ginger, minced
- ☐ 1 Tbs fresh turmeric, minced or 1–2 tsp curry powder
- ☐ 1 Tbs fresh garlic, minced
- ☐ 1 whole cinnamon stick
- ☐ 2 Tbs "Seed Spice Blend" (see page 86)
- ☐ 2 cups cooked chickpeas with cooking liquid*
- ☐ 4 cups "Potassium Broth" (see page 63) or water
- ☐ 1 tsp sea salt
- ☐ 2 cups fresh kale or spinach, chopped

1. Heat coconut oil in a large soup pot over medium heat.

2. Add onion, carrot, celery, and cubed squash. Sauté vegetables for 2–3 minutes until vegetables are slightly wilted, but not browned.

3. Add ginger, turmeric or curry powder, garlic, cinnamon stick, and "Seed Spice Blend" and stir to coat the vegetables with spices.

4. Add the cooked chickpeas with cooking liquid, "Potassium Broth" or water, and salt. Bring mixture to a boil and reduce heat to a simmer.

5. Cook about 15–20 minutes or until vegetables are cooked through and tender, adding more liquid if necessary.

6. Add greens and cook until wilted.

7. Remove cinnamon stick before serving and add more seasoning to taste.

See Cooking Beans, page 121

Serves 6

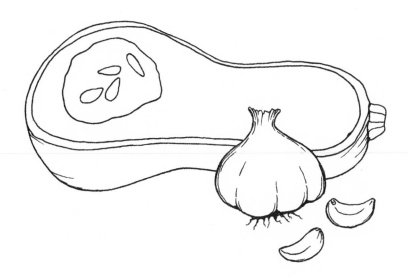

Snacks
Sauces
& Spices

Protein Power Smoothie

Great way to start your day in the morning or use to sustain your energy between meals throughout the day.

- [ ] One serving rice, hemp, or pea protein powder
- [ ] 1/2 cup fresh or frozen berries such as blueberries, straw-berries, or blackberries
- [ ] 1 heaping Tbs seed butter such as pumpkin, sesame, or sunflower
- [ ] About one cup of water

1. Add all ingredients to your blender and blend on high adding enough water to reach the desired consistency.

2. For added nutrition, add a large handful of greens such as spinach, cilantro, or chard.

Seed Spice Blend

Need to lower your cholesterol? Enjoy the sweet taste of coriander while supporting the liver in converting cholesterol to water–soluble bile.

- ☐ 1 ounce fenugreek seeds
- ☐ 1 ounce cumin seeds
- ☐ 1 ounce yellow mustard seeds
- ☐ 1 ounce fennel seeds
- ☐ 1 ounce coriander seeds

1. Mix raw seeds together and divide the mixture into two.

2. To toast seeds, place 1/2 seed blend mixture in a pre–heated dry skillet and gently stir until seeds begin to pop. Do not allow seeds to burn.

3. Remove seeds from hot pan and allow to cool before grinding.

4. Seeds can be ground in a coffee grinder or with a mortar and pestle prior to use.

Do not grind seeds to a fine powder.

Store both raw and toasted seeds in an airtight container.

Nori Gomasio

Beware! Many brands of Nori contain wheat. Wheat is added to many foods due to its binding properties. Read labels carefully whenever you buy a packaged product.

- ☐ 1 cup whole sesame seeds, hulls intact
- ☐ 2–3 sheets dried Laver or Nori
- ☐ 1 tsp sea salt

1. Cut or tear Laver sheets into small pieces, place in a mixing bowl, and set aside.

2. Heat a skillet to medium heat and add the sesame seeds and salt. Stir until seeds begin to pop and turn slightly brown. Do not burn.

3. Pour hot toasted seeds over torn Laver pieces in the mixing bowl and toss so hot seeds lightly toast the Laver.

4. Allow mixture to cool slightly and place in a food processor. Process until the seeds and Laver are coarsely ground.

Use Gomasio as a condiment to reduce salt and enhance flavor and nutrition in any recipe.

Makes about 1 cup

Olive & Herb Tapenade

The heart healthy oil in olives is also a great bile stimulator, increasing the liver's ability to clear toxins.

- ☐ 1 cup Kalamata olives, pitted
- ☐ 1/4 cup capers plus 1–2 Tbs caper juice
- ☐ 1–2 cloves garlic, finely minced
- ☐ 1/4 cup tightly packed basil leaves, chopped
- ☐ 1/4 cup tightly packed flat leaf parsley, chopped
- ☐ 2 Tbs olive oil
- ☐ 1–2 Tbs balsamic vinegar
- ☐ 1/4 tsp fresh ground black pepper

1. Place all ingredients into a food processor and pulse a few times.

2. Scrape down sides of work bowl and process a few more times.

3. Do not over–process.

Serve Tapenade as a dip with fresh vegetables or "Flax Crackers" (see page 102).

Kale & Sunflower Seed Pesto

This yummy side dish features kale, one of the cruciferous vegetable family members. Some other cruciferous veggies are: cabbage, broccoli, cauliflower, bok choy, rutabaga, and radish. This vegetable family is supportive of phase II liver function so should be eaten freely on a cleanse.

- ☐ 1 bunch kale, stemmed, washed, and coarsely chopped
- ☐ 1/2 tsp sea salt
- ☐ 2–3 cloves garlic, peeled and chopped
- ☐ 1/2 cup sunflower seeds, raw or toasted
- ☐ 1/4–1/2 cup extra virgin olive oil

1. Place about 1/2 inch of water in a medium saucepan with a tight fitting lid. Add kale and salt and cover.

2. Cook over medium heat until leaves are brightly colored and wilted, about 3–4 minutes. Do not overcook. Allow Kale to cool slightly and drain off any excess water.

3. Place cooked kale in a food processor with garlic and sunflower seeds. With the machine running, add the olive oil in a steady stream through the feed tube. Process until mixture is smooth and desired consistency is reached, occasionally scraping down processor bowl to evenly incorporate ingredients.

"Kale and Sunflower Seed Pesto" can be used in any dish calling for traditional pesto.

Makes about 1 cup

Cilantro & Pumpkin Seed Pesto

Cilantro has traditionally been used in removing metals such as lead and mercury from the body. High levels of these and other metals can cause damage to the brain and nervous system.

- ☐ 1/2 cup raw pumpkin seeds
- ☐ 1 large clove of garlic, minced
- ☐ 2 cups packed cilantro, washed, stems okay
- ☐ 1/4–1/2 cup olive oil
- ☐ Salt and pepper to taste

1. Place the pumpkin seeds and garlic in a food processor, and process until seeds and garlic are finely ground.

2. Place the cilantro into the food processor with the pumpkin seeds and garlic. With the machine running, add the olive oil in a steady stream through the feed tube. Process until mixture is smooth and desired consistency is reached, occasionally scraping down processor bowl to evenly incorporate ingredients.

3. Season pesto with salt and pepper to taste.

4. This pesto is wonderful to serve with "'Cured' Summer Squash & Herb Fettuccini" (see page 38).

5. Flat leaf parsley can be combined with, or used in place of, the cilantro.

Makes about 1 cup

Savory Tahini Sauce

Sesame seeds have multiple health benefits, including lowering of cholesterol and protecting all the cells of the body through their strong antioxidant properties.

- ☐ 2–3 Tbs coconut oil
- ☐ 1 cup onion, diced
- ☐ 2 cloves garlic, minced
- ☐ 1 Tbs fresh ginger, minced
- ☐ 1/4–1/2 cup tahini*, raw or roasted
- ☐ 1 Tbs ground cumin
- ☐ 2 Tbs toasted sesame oil
- ☐ 2 Tbs brown rice vinegar
- ☐ 1/4–1/2 cup water
- ☐ 1 tsp salt

1. Heat coconut oil in a saucepan over medium heat.

2. Add onion and sauté for 2–3 minutes, until slightly softened, but not browned. Add garlic and ginger and sauté for another minute or two.

3. Transfer onion mixture to a food processor or blender and add the tahini, cumin, sesame oil, brown rice vinegar, salt, and enough water to thin the mixture to desired consistency, adding more water if needed. Adjust seasoning before serving.

4. Sauce can be gently heated and served over steamed vegetables.

For a "raw" sauce, use raw tahini and sesame oil, omit sautéed onions, and use fresh garlic and ginger to flavor sauce.

Makes about 1 1/2 cups

Pumpkin & Sunflower
Seed Milk

Pumpkin seeds are a super source of zinc, a nutrient which protects our bodies from reactive oxygen intermediates also known as free radicals.

- ☐ 1/2 cup raw pumpkin seeds soaked overnight and drained
- ☐ 1/2 cup raw sunflower seeds soaked overnight and drained
- ☐ 1/2 cup raw white sesame seeds (optional)
- ☐ 4 cups water
- ☐ Scant pinch of sea salt

1. In a blender, combine soaked seeds, water, and salt.

2. Blend until mixture is smooth and seeds are ground.

3. The mixture can be strained (or not) at this point and used as a milk substitute.

Makes about 1 quart

Brown Rice
& Vegetable Nori Rolls

Looking for more cruciferous veggies to promote phase II liver pathways? Include arugula in this tasty snack.

☐ Cooked "Brown Sushi Rice"*
☐ 1–package dried Nori sheets
☐ Bamboo sushi mat

Any of the following:
☐ 2 cups baby Arugula or spinach
☐ 1 cup fresh sprouts (any kind)
☐ 1 cup grated carrots
☐ 1/2 cup grated Daikon radish
☐ 1/2 cup grated jicama
☐ 1/4 cup thinly sliced red onion
☐ Avocado slices (optional)
☐ Any fresh leafy herbs like cilantro, basil, or parsley, chopped
☐ Sesame seeds for garnish

1. Place a sheet of Nori on bamboo mat. Dampen hands to prevent rice from sticking and evenly flatten a handful (about 1 cup) of the "Brown Sushi Rice" onto a sheet of Nori.

2. Place some Arugula and any combination of sprouts, grated or sliced vegetables, avocado, and herbs in a line, onto the center of the bed of rice and roll up.

3. Cut rolls crosswise into serving sizes, and garnish with sesame seeds.

Makes 4–6 rolls

For the "Brown Sushi Rice":
- ☐ 2 cups short grain brown rice
- ☐ 5 cups water
- ☐ 1/2 tsp salt
- ☐ 1/4 – 1/2 cup brown rice vinegar
- ☐ 1 tsp sea salt

1. In a medium saucepot, bring rice, water, and salt to a boil. Reduce heat to a simmer, cover with a tight fitting lid, and cook for 45–55 minutes, or until all the water is absorbed and the rice is cooked. Allow rice to rest 10 minutes before removing the lid.

2. While rice is cooking, in a small bowl, mix brown rice vinegar and salt.

3. When rice is done resting but still warm, stir in the vinegar and salt mixture.

4. Set "Brown Sushi Rice" aside for Nori rolls.

Makes about 4 cups

Pacific Wakamemole

*Concerned about lead toxicity? Calcium competes
with lead at binding sites thereby reducing its
toxic effect. Seaweed is an excellent source of
calcium to enjoy on your cleanse.*

- ☐ 2 medium sized ripe avocados, pit removed and peeled
- ☐ 1 large clove of garlic, smashed and finely minced
- ☐ 2–4 Tbs red onion, finely minced
- ☐ 2–4 Tbs Pacific Wakame seaweed, rinsed and soaked according to directions on package and drained thoroughly
- ☐ 1/4 cup cilantro, chopped
- ☐ 2 Tbs apple cider or brown rice vinegar
- ☐ Salt and pepper to taste

1. Place avocados in a mixing bowl and mash with a fork to desired consistency.

2. Add in remaining ingredients and mix until combined.

3. Taste and add more salt, pepper, or vinegar if desired.

Serve with fresh vegetables or "Flax Crackers" (see page 102).

Serves 4

Roasted Spiced Chick Peas

Black pepper contains the phytonutrient piperine, a nutrient supportive of liver detoxification.

- ☐ 2 cups "Ginger and Kombu Chickpeas"* cooked and drained
- ☐ 2–4 Tbs extra virgin olive oil
- ☐ 1 tsp ground cumin
- ☐ 1/2 tsp ground coriander
- ☐ 1/2 tsp granulated garlic
- ☐ 1/2 tsp black pepper
- ☐ 1/2 tsp sea salt

1. Pre–heat oven to 400 degrees F.

2. Lightly oil baking sheet with 1 Tbs olive oil.

3. In a mixing bowl, combine 2 cups cooked and drained "Ginger and Kombu Chickpeas" (along with some softened pieces of Kombu seaweed and ginger), the spices, and enough olive oil to coat the chickpeas.

4. Place seasoned chickpea and spice mixture in a single layer on the prepared baking sheet and bake for 20–30 minutes, turning occasionally until they are crisp and golden.

For Ginger and Kombu Chickpeas:
- ☐ 2 cups dried chickpeas, soaked overnight and drained
- ☐ 2–3 slices of fresh ginger
- ☐ 2–3 1–inch pieces of Kombu seaweed
- ☐ 6–8 cups of water
- ☐ 1 tsp salt

1. Place soaked, drained chickpeas, ginger, Kombu seaweed and water into a large pot.

2. Bring to a boil, reduce heat to low, cover and simmer for 1 1/2 to 2 hours, or until chickpeas are tender, adding salt halfway through cooking or after chickpeas have softened.

3. Allow mixture to cool and drain chickpeas for roasting, reserving any extra chickpeas or cooking liquid for soups or stews.

Makes about 2 1/2 cups

Raw Vegetable & Sunflower Seed Pate

> *Sunflowers are a rich source of vitamin E, the body's primary fat soluble antioxidant.*

- [ ] 2 cups sunflower seeds, soaked for 2–4 hours, or overnight, and drained
- [ ] 2–4 Tbs apple cider vinegar
- [ ] 1 carrot, chopped (about 1 cup)
- [ ] 1 stalk of celery, chopped (about 1 cup)
- [ ] 1/4 cup green onions, chopped
- [ ] 1/4 cup flat leaf parsley, chopped
- [ ] 1 small clove garlic, minced
- [ ] 1 Tbs mustard seeds
- [ ] 1 tsp kelp (optional)
- [ ] Salt and pepper to taste

Place all ingredients in a food processor and process to a smooth paste.

Taste for seasoning and serve with raw vegetables or "Flax Crackers" (see page 102).

Makes about 4 cups

White Bean Kale & Garlic Dip

This is a great recipe to keep handy in the fridge for those times when hunger strikes and you are unprepared.

- ☐ 2 cups "cooked" white navy or Great Northern beans cooked with Kombu seaweed and ginger (see basic bean recipe)
- ☐ 1 bunch kale, stemmed, washed, and coarsely chopped
- ☐ 2–3 cloves garlic, peeled and chopped
- ☐ 1/2 tsp salt
- ☐ 1/4 cup extra virgin olive oil (optional)
- ☐ White pepper to taste

1. Place about 1/2 inch of water in a medium saucepan with a tight fitting lid. Add kale, garlic, and salt and cover.

2. Cook kale over medium heat until leaves are brightly colored and wilted, about 3–4 minutes. Do not overcook. Allow Kale to cool slightly and drain off any excess water.

3. Place cooked kale in a food processor, with the cooked navy, or other white bean, and some pieces of the cooked ginger and softened Kombu seaweed. With the machine running, add the olive oil (if using) in a steady stream through the feed tube.

4. Process until mixture is smooth and desired consistency is reached, occasionally scraping down processor bowl to evenly incorporate ingredients. If not using oil, a bit of the bean cooking liquid will substitute.

Season mixture with more salt and pepper if desired. Serve as dip with fresh vegetables or "Flax Crackers" (see page 102).

Makes about 2 1/2 cups

Yellow Split Pea Dahl
with Black Mustard Seeds

Got too much gas? Small beans such as split peas,
mung beans, and lentils are easier to digest
due to the smaller amount of fiber.

- ☐ 1 cup yellow split peas
- ☐ 1 Tbs fresh ginger, peeled and minced
- ☐ 2 cloves fresh garlic, minced
- ☐ 1 Tbs fresh turmeric, minced or 1 tsp ground
- ☐ 1/2 tsp salt
- ☐ 2 green onions, chopped
- ☐ 2–3 tsp black mustard seeds
- ☐ White pepper to taste

1. Sort through peas to remove any small stones, rinse well, and cover with water.

2. Allow peas to soak for about two to four hours before cooking. Pour off soaking water and rinse again.

3. Place soaked, drained split peas in a pot and add 3 cups of fresh water, the ginger, garlic, turmeric, and salt.

4. Bring to a boil, reduce heat to low, cover and simmer for 35–45 minutes, stirring occasionally, until peas are completely soft and cooked through.

5. Allow mixture to cool and blend to a puree. Season puree with salt and pepper to taste. To serve, top with green onions and black mustard seeds.

Serve Dahl as a dip with fresh vegetables or "Flax Crackers" (see page 102).

Makes about 2 cups

Ginger & Kombu Seaweed Hummus

It is always important to have a quick snack handy to avoid reaching for convenience foods when you are really hungry. Hummus is great with fresh veggies and can tide you over as you prepare your next meal.

- ☐ 2 cups cooked "Ginger and Kombu Chickpeas" (see page 97) drained with cooking liquid reserved
- ☐ 1/4 cup raw sesame tahini
- ☐ 2 to 3 cloves fresh garlic, minced
- ☐ 2–4 Tbs apple cider vinegar
- ☐ 1/2 tsp salt

1. Place all ingredients, except the cooking liquid, in a food processor. Include some of the softened Kombu seaweed and pieces of ginger from the cooked chickpeas.

2. Process mixture while slowly adding only enough of the cooking liquid until mixture is smooth and creamy and reaches the desired consistency.

3. Add more salt, vinegar, or garlic to taste.

Serve Hummus with fresh cut raw vegetables, "Flax Crackers" (see page 102), baked Mochi* or "Steamed Artichoke" (see page 25).

*Mochi is a Japanese glutinous rice cake which comes in many flavors. Mochi rice cakes and Kombu seaweed are available at health food stores or Asian markets. Mochi is gluten free.

Makes about 3 Cups

Flax Crackers

Flax seed is rich in lignans which have been shown to reduce the risk of colon cancer.

☐ 1 cup brown or golden flax seeds
☐ 1/2 cup sunflower seeds
☐ 1/4 cup sesame seeds
☐ 1 cup onion, chopped
☐ 1 cup cucumber, chopped
☐ 1/4 cup or more of pure filtered water
☐ 1 tsp sea salt

1. Preheat oven to 250 degrees.

2. Place all the ingredients in a food processor and process until combined. The mixture should be moist and easy to spread. Add more water if necessary.

3. Evenly spread the seed mixture to about a 1/4 inch thickness onto an oiled cookie sheet and score into squares.

4. Slowly bake for about 1 hour or until crackers are dried and crisp.

For a more flavorful cracker, add spices or herbs, like fresh ginger, garlic, and basil, or caraway and coriander seeds to the mix. You can also add other vegetables such as celery and grated carrots as long as your final mixture remains a little moist. Even use apples and dates for a sweet cracker.

For a "raw" cracker, spread mixture onto dehydrator trays and follow dehydrator instructions.

Desserts

Summer Fruits *with Balsamic Syrup*

> *"Stone fruit" is any fruit with a stony pit. These fruits are meant to be eaten in abundance when in season. Eating fresh foods in season is a great way to stay in sync with the environment.*

- ☐ 3–4 cups seasonal, ripe stone fruits: like peaches, plums, apricots, and/or nectarines, etc, rinsed, pits removed, and cut into pieces
- ☐ 4 Tbs Balsamic Syrup*
- ☐ 8 fresh basil leaves, cut into ribbons

1. Divide cut fruits into four dessert bowls and drizzle each with about 1 Tbs of the cooled Balsamic Syrup.
2. Top with ribbons of basil.

Serves 4

Balsamic syrup:
1. Place 2 cups of balsamic vinegar in a non corrosive saucepot over medium–low heat and gently simmer until vinegar is reduced in volume by half, to about 1 cup. Be careful not to burn.
2. Allow syrup to cool to room temperature.

Balsamic Syrup can also be used as a salad dressing along with a little olive oil.

Makes about 1 cup

Green Apple & Pomegranate Salad
with Cinnamon Tahini Sauce

Pomegranates are high in polyphenol compounds, phytonutrients which decrease "silent inflammation" associated with cancer, heart disease, and diabetes.

- ☐ 2 large or 4 small green (or other) apples, unpeeled, cored and sliced
- ☐ Seeds from 1 pomegranate
- ☐ 1/2 cup Cinnamon Tahini Sauce*
- ☐ 8 fresh mint leaves, cut into ribbons

1. In a mixing bowl, toss together apple slices and pomegranate seeds.

2. Divide the "Apple and Pomegranate Salad" into 4 dessert bowls and top with Cinnamon Tahini Sauce.

3. Garnish with the ribbons of mint and an extra dusting of cinnamon.

Cinnamon Tahini Sauce:
- ☐ 1/2 cup raw sesame tahini
- ☐ 1 Tbs ginger, peeled, grated, or finely minced
- ☐ 1 tsp cinnamon
- ☐ 1 tsp vanilla extract
- ☐ 1/2 tsp almond extract
- ☐ 2 to 4 Tbs water

1. In a mixing bowl, whisk together the tahini, ginger, cinnamon, vanilla and almond extracts.

2. Whisk in only enough water to thin the tahini to the desired sauce consistency.

3. Adjust seasoning to taste.

Makes about ¾ cup

Coconut & Ginger Roasted Pears

> *Flax seeds are high in the plant fiber lignan which bind estrogens. Estrogen is frequently in excess in both men and women due to estrogens found in our food and water.*

- ☐ 4 seasonally ripe pears* of your choice, unpeeled, quartered, and cored
- ☐ 2–3 Tbs coconut oil, melted
- ☐ 1 Tbs fresh ginger, finely minced or 1 tsp ground
- ☐ 1/4 tsp nutmeg
- ☐ 2 Tbs ground flax seeds mixed with 1/4 tsp cinnamon, cardamom, and/or nutmeg

1. Preheat oven to 350 degrees F.

2. In a mixing bowl, toss together quartered pears, melted coconut oil, ginger, and nutmeg until combined.

3. Place pear mixture in a shallow baking dish in a single layer and bake for 20 to 25 minutes, or until pears are tender and golden but still hold their shape. Do not overcook.

4. Divide roasted pears into serving bowls and top with ground flax seed and spice mixture.

*Apples can be substituted for the pears.

Serves 4

Three Flavored Summer Fruit Skewers

Mint is a fabulous digestive aid. It reduces gassiness and increases bile flow thereby assisting the liver in removing toxins.

☐ Any combination of seasonally ripe stone fruit, melons and/or strawberries, cut into one–inch pieces, pits and seeds removed, and totaling 4 cups
☐ 1 Tbs vanilla extract
☐ 1/2 tsp anise or almond extract
☐ 8–10 6" bamboo skewers
☐ 1 Tbs mint leaves, cut into ribbons

1. Toss cut fruit and berries with seasonings to coat. Add more or less extracts to taste.

2. Skewer seasoned fruit onto bamboo skewers, alternating fruits and berries.

3. Top skewers with ribbons of mint, and serve.

Makes about 8–10 skewers

Baked Cinnamon & Sesame Apples

> *Not only is cinnamon yummy, it also has anti–inflamma-tory and antioxidant properties. In addition, it stabilized blood sugar, making it the perfect spice in sweet dishes.*

- ☐ 4 medium red delicious or other seasonally ripe apples, unpeeled and cored
- ☐ 2–3 Tbs white or hulled sesame seeds
- ☐ 2 Tbs melted coconut oil
- ☐ 1–2 tsp cinnamon
- ☐ 1 Tbs mint, cut into ribbons for garnish

1. Preheat oven to 350 degrees F.

2. In a mixing bowl, toss together sesame seeds, melted coconut oil, and cinnamon.

3. Fill cored apples with sesame seed mixture.

4. Place stuffed apples in a shallow baking dish with an inch or so of water. Cover and bake stuffed apples for 40–50 minutes, or until apples are tender and softened but still hold their shape.

5. Allow Baked Apples to cool and top with ribbons of mint

Serves 4

Rose Flavored Berry Medley

Berries are rich in the phytonutrient anthocyanin. This nutrient increases the concentration of Vitamin C in our cells and protects against free radicals, especially in the brain.

- [ ] 4 cups of any combination of mixed seasonal berries like blueberries, raspberries, blackberries, or strawberries. (Frozen berries are OK)
- [ ] 1 tsp vanilla extract or 1/2 tsp almond extract
- [ ] 1/2 tsp Rosewater*
- [ ] Mint leaves cut into ribbons for garnish

1. In a mixing bowl, gently toss together the mixed berries with the vanilla and/or almond extracts and the Rosewater until combined.

2. Divide the berry mixture into 4 dessert bowls and top with a sprinkling of mint.

Rosewater is available at Middle Eastern or Specialty food markets.

Serves 4

Ginger Spiced Apple Sauté

Suffering from a sweet tooth? Vanilla is a sweet tasting flavor which can nurture the child inside who may just need some comfort food.

- ☐ 2–3 Tbs coconut oil, melted
- ☐ 2 large or 4 small seasonally ripe apples*, unpeeled, cored, and sliced
- ☐ 1 Tbs fresh ginger, peeled and finely minced
- ☐ 1 tsp vanilla extract
- ☐ 1/2 tsp cinnamon
- ☐ 1/4 tsp ground nutmeg
- ☐ 1 Tbs mint, cut into thin strips
- ☐ 1 Tbs Hemp seeds (optional)

1. Heat a skillet over medium–high heat, and add the coconut oil, apples, and ginger.

2. Sauté apples for 2–3 minutes until slightly wilted and browned. Allow to cool.

3. Add the vanilla extract, cinnamon, and the ground nutmeg. Toss to coat the apples with the spices.

4. To serve, divide apples into four bowls and top with mint and hemp seeds.

*Seasonally ripe pears can be substituted for the apples.

Serves 4

Baked Pumpkin Spiced Sweet Potato Whip

Nutmeg is very high in mystericin, a phytonutrient which has been shown to be strongly protective of liver cells.

- [ ] 2 large baked sweet potatoes, peeled (about 4 cups total)
- [ ] 1 Tbs vanilla extract
- [ ] 1/2 tsp almond extract
- [ ] 1–2 tsp ground cinnamon
- [ ] 1/4 tsp ground nutmeg
- [ ] 1/4 tsp ground coriander
- [ ] 1/4 tsp ground cloves
- [ ] 1/4 tsp ground cardamom

1. Place the peeled baked sweet potato, along with any or all of the spices, in a food processor.

2. Puree until well blended and smooth. Taste for seasoning and add more spices if desired.

3. "Spiced Sweet Potato Whip" can be served at this point or transferred to a shallow baking dish and baked at 350 degrees for 25–30 minutes or until golden and bubbly.

Serves 4

Cleansing Effects of Foods & Spices

The Cleansing Effects
of Foods & Spices

Anise, Caraway, Cardamon, Coriander, and Dill are spices used medicinally as carminatives which ease intestinal colic, flatulence and gripping. The increase in fiber in the cleanse diet may cause digestive upset which can be reduced with using these herbs.

Artichoke is a liver tonic and restorative, making it a perfect cleanse food. It stimulates bile and reduces blood lipids by enhancing cholesterol metabolism.

Cinnamon is warming to the digestive tract. Cinnamon is useful in colon cleansing as it decreases spasm caused by herbs, clay, and charcoal; substances often used in cleanse programs. It is antibacterial and antifungal, making it useful in balancing the bacterial flora, which live in the intestines.

Cloves are extremely warming to the digestive system and can be helpful on a detox program when the bowels become cold and sluggish.

Dark leafy greens are known in naturopathic medicine as the liver's best friend and have long been hailed as liver tonics in Chinese medicine. The secret may lie in the abundance of nutrients such as vitamins A, C, E, and K, folic acid, calcium, magnesium, iron, potassium, phosphorous, and zinc. Many of these nutrients are essential to the metabolic pathways performed by the liver.

Fennel Seeds are relaxing to the intestines, preventing and relieving intestinal cramping and flatulence. Fennel supports cleansing through regeneration of liver cells. In addition, fennel reduces inflammation in the intestines.

Fenugreek has historically been used in herbal formulas to lower blood sugar and reduce the craving for sweet foods. It is a digestive aid and has been shown to heal stomach ulcers.

Garlic is a strong antibacterial and antiparasitic food, supporting the development of natural bacterial flora while killing pathogenic organisms. It reduces cholesterol and opens the skin channel by stimulating a sweat.

Ginger is a gastric tonic that relieves indigestion and nausea. Ginger is protective of the liver and helps to lower cholesterol.

Peppermint is one of the best culinary carminatives. Carminatives are relaxing to the bowels and reduce intestinal gas and cramping. Peppermint also stimulates bile. Peppermint increases sweating thereby opening the skin channel during the detox process.

Rosemary is stimulating to the digestion, the liver, and the gall bladder. It increases the flow of bile and reduces flatulence. It is antifungal and antibacterial, helping to keep the gut flora in balance.

Turmeric is a favored herb in cleansing as it supports so many of the goals of detoxification. First, it is protective to the cells of the liver. As toxins are mobilized and converted to benign waste by the liver, turmeric helps protect the liver from these toxins.

In addition, turmeric mobilizes and increases the solubility of bile. Bile is produced by the liver, stored in the gall bladder, and is important in fat digestion. When the liver is sluggish, the cholesterol in bile can become lumpy and form gallstones. Turmeric assists in detoxification by cleaning out the gall bladder.

Finally, turmeric is a potent antioxidant, as effective as vitamin C and vitamin E. An antioxidant protects cells from oxidation reactions, which can produce free radicals. Free radicals start chain reactions that damage cells.

Food Preparation Tips

Cooking Beans
and the
Nuts & Bolts
of Nuts & Seeds

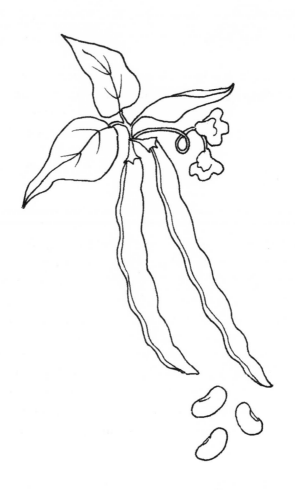

Cooking Beans

Soaking the beans and other legumes prior to cooking reduces cooking time and removes some of the indigestible sugars that cause flatulence.

To soak the beans, add 3–4 cups of water per cup of beans. Do not add salt or anything else at this time. The best time to soak your beans is overnight or first thing in the morning of the day you want to cook the beans. In my family, eating the last of the pot of beans is the cue for starting a new batch soaking.

A good soak takes about 8 hours. Lentils and split peas need only soak for 30–60 minutes (can soak longer) and only need about 1 1/2 cups of water per cup of soaked beans.

Stovetop cooking requires no additional cooking accessories. It remains the most popular method of cooking beans.

When beans have been pre–soaked, they require 1–4 hours of cooking time with small beans such as Mung beans and Black Eyed Peas cooking the fastest, and Garbanzo beans taking the longest.

When the soak is complete, discard the water, rinse the beans, and add new cooking water. Add enough water to bring the level in the pot a couple of inches above the soaked beans. Bring to a boil, skim off the white foamy froth, and reduce to a simmer, cooking until tender. Removing foam during the boiling stage further reduces gas–forming sugars. Stir occasionally and add more water as needed.

Pressure cooking is a great choice for families that have less time to finish the cooking process.

Drain the beans and add water to cover the beans. Do not fill greater than a third of the pot as beans will need room to expand. Adding a tablespoon of coconut oil will reduce foaming. Cooking time is reduced to 25–30 minutes.

Be sure to follow the directions on your cooker as they can vary. Do not cook beans with skins such as fava, lima, and lupini as the skins may clog the vent.

Crock–Pots are also a great tool used to reduce cooking time. As with the other methods, drain and replace the water. For families who do not suffer from gas when eating beans, crock–pots can be used overnight with un–soaked beans.

Use 3–4 cups of water per cup of beans. Fill the crock pot one–third with beans and water, bring to a boil on high, and then reduce to the lowest setting. Wake in the morning to the smell of fresh cooked beans!

Flavors and Salt has specific times to be added in the cooking process. Salt and acids, such as lemon, tomato, or vinegar, should be added at the end of the cooking process when the beans are tender. If added earlier these flavorings can lengthen the cooking time and prevent the bean from properly softening.

Garlic, onion, Kombu seaweed and mint can be added after the soak when cooking the beans. The addition of these popular bean condiments will add flavor and increase the digestibility of beans. They may be used alone or in combination as desired by the cook. Per 2 cups of dry beans, use half an onion, 1–2 cloves of garlic, 1 piece of Kombu and/or a sprig of fresh mint.

Nuts & Bolts of Nuts & Seeds

Buying and storing nuts and seeds are the first two steps in ensuring freshness and avoiding rancidity.

Nuts should be whole, not chopped, and are best if sold from a cooler rather than at room temperature. Cutting up nuts prior to use and heating nuts both lead to rancidity.

When you get them home, remove nuts and seeds from bags and store in glass, preferably in the refrigerator. Do not chop or grind the nuts and seeds until you are ready to use them in cooking.

Tree nuts are any nuts that grow on a tree. This includes walnuts, almonds, hazelnuts, Brazil nuts, cashews, coconut, pecans, pine nuts, macadamia nuts, pistachios, lichee nuts, and chestnuts.

Tree nut allergies tend to cause significant acute responses such as hives, breathing difficulties, and swelling, so most people are aware if they have a nut allergy. However, many people have more subtle intolerance symptoms, which is why we ask you to eliminate nuts for the duration of at least one cleanse, challenging them after your cleanse to see if they cause any problems for you.

Seeds which are fine to eat even if you have a nut allergy are: sunflower, chia, flax, mustard, pumpkin, squash, caraway, radish, alfalfa, dill, clover, fenugreek, cabbage, kale, poppy, and pomegranate. Sesame seeds do sometimes cause reactions in people who have tree nut allergies.

Soaking of nuts improves digestion

Raw nuts contain enzyme inhibitors which block enzymes, making nuts more difficult to digest. Soaking for a couple of hours or overnight can remove these inhibitors and improve digestion.

To get the crunch back, you can dry them in a food dryer or in the oven at 200 degrees with the door open until dry (about 15–20 minutes).

Sprouting nuts and seeds can assist in digestion and increase the nutritional value of these great foods.

Sprouts are living food and high in enzymes, which help the intestines get the most out of what we eat. Sprouting also makes the nutrients in nuts and seeds more readily available.

Visit livingfoods.com for specific soaking and sprouting methods for a variety of seeds, nuts, grains, and beans.

Roasting nuts and seeds can enhance their flavor and their texture and can make a good treat.

We recommend roasting nuts and seeds in the oven at 160–170 degrees for 15–20 minutes right before you eat them.

You want to avoid eating roasted nuts which have been stored because they have a greater chance of becoming rancid.

Low–heat roasted nuts are better because the fats in nuts heated at a high temperature will be damaged and begin a process called lipid peroxidation. Oxidized fats can then damage structural fats in our cell membranes anywhere in the body.

Toasting Seeds: Heat a dry skillet over medium heat and add seeds. Gently stir until seeds begin to pop and are lightly browned and aromatic. Remove toasted seeds from hot pan to prevent burning.

Shopping List

Spices & Flavoring
Beans, Grains & Seeds
Fats & Condiments
Vegetables & Fruit

Spices and Flavoring

Dried

- [ ] Bay Leaves
- [ ] Basil
- [ ] Black Pepper
- [ ] Cardamon
- [ ] Cumin Seeds
- [ ] Coriander
- [ ] Fennel Seeds
- [ ] Fenugreek
- [ ] Mustard Seeds
- [ ] Oregano
- [ ] Rosemary
- [ ] Sea Salt
- [ ] Thyme
- [ ] Turmeric Powder

Fresh

- [ ] Basil
- [ ] Dill
- [ ] Garlic
- [ ] Ginger
- [ ] Mint
- [ ] Turmeric

Beans, Grains & Seeds

Beans

- [ ] Adzuki Beans
- [ ] Black Beans
- [ ] Black-eyed Peas
- [ ] Chick Peas
- [ ] French Lentils
- [ ] Lima Beans
- [ ] Mung Beans
- [ ] Pinto Beans
- [ ] White Beans

Grains

- ☐ Amaranth
- ☐ Basmati Rice
- ☐ Millet
- ☐ Quinoa
- ☐ Short Grain Brown Rice
- ☐ Teff

Seeds

- ☐ Black Sesame Seeds
- ☐ Pumpkin Seeds
- ☐ Sunflower Seeds
- ☐ Sesame Seeds

Fats & Condiments

Oils

- ☐ Virgin Coconut Oil
- ☐ Extra Virgin Olive Oil
- ☐ Toasted Sesame Oil
- ☐ Olives

Vinegars

- ☐ Balsamic Vinegar
- ☐ Red Wine Vinegar
- ☐ Umeboshi Plum Vinegar

Vegetables & Fruits

Fresh vegetables, spices, and fruits should be purchased as you need them. Plan your weekly menu and make a list of desired produce. Be flexible, as what is on your list may not be available, while great looking fresh alternatives are.

Fresh Vegetables in Season

In general, a cleanse in the Spring would call for fresh baby greens and sprouts while a Fall cleanse would benefit from root vegetables and squashes. Keep in mind that the more we eat foods in season, the more we benefit from their inherent properties.

Sea Vegetables
☐ Kombu seaweed
☐ Nori (check label, make sure wheat–free)
☐ Arame
☐ Hijiki
☐ Wakame seaweed

Fresh Fruit
☐ Apples
☐ Berries: Blackberries, Boysenberries, Marionberries, Raspberries, Strawberries
☐ Figs
☐ Pears
☐ Stone fruit: Apricots, Cherries, Nectarines, Peaches, Plums

Frozen Fruit
☐ Berries
☐ Cherries

About the Authors

DR. BONNIE NEDROW practices naturopathic medicine at Hidden Springs Wellness Center in Ashland, Oregon. Her passion is to educate and inspire her clients to build strong preventive health habits and to learn how to care for themselves when an illness does occur. At the core of this education is an understanding of the ability of the body to heal, especially when provided a healthy diet and lifestyle.

Dr. Nedrow specializes in Environmental Medicine, a new field linking the effects of chemical toxins to human disease. Her main focus is on the health of children and to this end she has developed a preconception program to help couples to attain optimal health with a low toxic load prior to conceiving their children. She also sees clients of all ages, leading many of them through detoxification programs to help them restore health.

She is coauthor with Dr. Rod Newton of *The Seasonal Cleanse Workbook*, available at HiddenSpringsWellness.com.

CHEF JEFF HAUPTMAN is a 30-year veteran of the restaurant and catering industry. A native New Yorker, he worked his culinary magic in San Diego before relocating to Ashland, Oregon, where he is well-known for his elegant and healthy menus. In 2004, Jeff learned of a diabetic condition that changed his personal approach to food and lifestyle choices. He lost 55 pounds while becoming well-versed in creating exciting gourmet recipes for a variety of therapeutic, nutritional, and special diets, including low glycemic, salt free, gluten free, and dairy free cooking. His work has been acknowledged in Oprah Winfrey's diet cookbook, and in *The Healthy Kitchen*, a cookbook by Dr. Andrew Weil. The Gerson Institute has also acknowledged his contribution in preparing their therapeutic recipes.